Concrete in Watercolor

Lancelot Schaubert

Cover design by Lancelot Schaubert

Schaubert, Lancelot

CONCRETE IN WATERCOLOR / Lancelot Schaubert

ISBN: 9781949547245

POETRY / Subjects & Themes / Places

POETRY / Subjects & Themes / Political & Protest

POETRY / Subjects & Themes / Death, Grief, Loss

Printed in the United States of America

Contents

Introduction

"For if syllabic verse is like carving in wood and *vers libre* like working with a brush, this is like carving in granite." — Jack Lewis

I spent almost the entirety of my last poetry anthology focusing on the alliterative meter — on carving in granite while focusing on the romantic nature of Greenwood Cemetery's leaves and trees and fish. (I will forever refuse to use their foundation's mid word dash). All romanticism of the woods connected to that necropolis metaphor forced its way into that anthology from the Hudson line on the MTA north to my last visit to Greenville, Ohio. My future poetic endeavors, I think, will continually add to that project until it swells larger than *Leaves of Grass*, constantly revising and giving it new versions over and over again so that people can see the progress of a poetic life. That's how Whitman did it and things worked out okay for him. They're the subjects I care about most — love, death, nature, prayer — so I feel no need to venture forth any further from that metaphor. Riffing will be sufficient for me. After this volume, I will return to Greenwood and make a happy home there forever. It will probably be excessive, the sheer number of versions, but when am I not excessive? There's optimism and then there's optimal living, as Bradbury said. I prefer to live my days in such a way that they remember eternity to come. That transcendence breaks in with the dawn, the dusk, and the dust of Brooklyn.

In this volume, I wanted to invert both foci of the last: I wish to paint with watercolors and carve with wood rather than to carve in granite, as Lewis would have it, and make my subject matter focusing on the concrete of the city rather than the leaves and birds of the field. This antinomy of both — a stone sculpture of the Fae; a watercolor of concrete — proves to me illuminating in a way similar to Wordsworth's and Coleridge's project. *Concrete in Watercolor* lead me into surrealism, back to Greenwood, and everywhere in between.

It's also, because I cannot seem to get the practice of the alliterative meter out of my head, ended up reverting to the mean of alliterative meter. This pleased Paul Deane, the editor of Forgotten Ground Regained (who, as of this revision, will be crashing on my couch in order to share a table with me at the NYC poetry festival). But I'm happy to say I've bracketed all of those poems off at the end into a separate section entitled "reversion to the mean."

Perhaps it's something like a synthesis?

A way in which I am now sculpting in granite what I modeled in wood after having studied in watercolor the place where grass pierces concrete and bedrock holds up grass?

I take heart in this antinomy and revision to the mean. It would be like if my friend Abraham Mohler stopped sculpting for a year to paint and then realized that, however fun, he liked sculpting more after all.

Lastly, though these poems were published in many places — *Forgotten Ground Regained* and *Space and Time* and *Life in a Time of Covid* and *Alliteration* and *Teach. Write.* etc. — I opted out of my typical "originally published in x" beneath the title or even at the end. I'm going to move that way more and more. I suppose if you really care to see where something was published, you can check the published works page on my website. But that's more work for an archivist or academic than for the average poetry reader. Most people do not care. Most people *should not* care.

There are two reasons for the my decision. The first is that it gets you straight into the poem without the distraction of me having one eye on the prestige or credentials. The second is that some of my favorite poems are poems unpublished until I self-publish them either on my site or in a book like this. The third is that some of the poems that have lived on were self-published and many that have died on the refuse of history were originally lauded by the academy. Both the public and the elite get things wrong, you see. So why bias anyone in any way? That I publish new poems alongside credentialed poems should add legitimacy to those unpublished. That I publish credentialed poems alongside new poems should add freshness and publicity to those already lauded. Refusing to mention whether or not one sold will force you into the poetic version of a cross-caste mixer.

You and you alone, therefore, will determine what's good and what will live on. What do the editors know?

No offense, Paul. But then again, you have taken more of my poems than any two editors combined, so I doubt you'll hate much in here.

I do so hate high society *per se* — though I love many specific friends within high society — and so I would much rather watch the children of Brooklyn paint with watercolors upon the places where the rich paved over paradise.

And so here is *Concrete in Watercolor*, with a reversion to the mean of alliteration at the end and an eye for my eventual return to Greenwood's fairy castle...

— Lancelot Schaubert

38th Birthday (having again doubled my age and written at least 74 poems at 37)

[I had breakfast at DnD diner — apple cinnamon pancakes — a sticky bun from Baked in Brooklyn, jerk chicken from the fellas with the smoker outside the Apple Store, and a spindrift here in—]

Downtown Brooklyn
Center for Fiction
4:06pm
2025

Last, The Shadows

You begin with a wash
Perhaps of periwinkle
Streaks of invisible slate
Behind it, another of sand; dandelion
bleached
Before: fresh dried scab
It's the shadows you have to add
Not the light
The light has been there since before St.
Anthony
Who left the urban lamppost on a hill
Seven hills, then, seven left
To take it to the gates of hell
It's an offensive thing to say
To go on the attack where the wyrms and
wyverns slither lowdune
To sunder Ourborous's lemniscate hole and
take it to the
Wilder
Nessie
That's where you'll find the dark.

The city's awash with the cousin of the cave,
It's the shadows you add in later, on top,
Hint of sun hit if you and the neighbor boys
Accidentally knock a stickball too high over
the towers into
Neighbor Greenwood's yard.
Last, you'll have to add in
The old windowsills where the folk fled the
falling towers
Score marks from brimstone noose ghosts
The rust stains where the great hotel met
Controlled demolition
Between Gallery House
And blackface whiskey trader (again, added
later)
The midtown fire hydrants and parking
meters
Sable pants that hide mudstains
SUVs of foreign dignitaries bartering their
poor for your poor
Nipple stickies
Oscar bases
The followers overshadowing the foundry of
thought
Black tie affairs, black AMEX, blackout sales
Scaffolding on scaffolding on scaffolding
hidden
in same eld black fishnet from ye drag
queen hide
(Not the brazen, naked kind my father and
Remmy built)
((Scaffolds, I mean: you have to clarify here))
(((For them, at least)))
((((My father and Remmy, I mean))))
(((((their light, then fishnet, fishers, then
fishers of men, only then — only then —

men fish caught in their own
costumes)))))

You start with a wash.

Everything else rides the coattails of white
canvas.
A 1970's tuxedo on a 35-year old virgin
groom who was the best men for all of his
groomsmen.
That's a city.

Now.
Dear desert,
Thou mayst now throw thy tar.
Yet, mid-pitch, remember, whatever its tra-
jectory,
That the Buddha said it's rather hard to kick
A possessive pronoun.
If we refuse to receive your gift of tar,
To whom does the gift belong?

Manhattanhenge

Bricks blind you
Not by the overreach of the thrown
(Though that too, they can,
They Can)
But in the evening on sixth avenue
In the winter where the light
Hugs the winter solstice side
of Manhattanhenge
And reflects off a yellowbrick road to heaven
The fiat currency fades
Gold comes of pre-modern edifice
Long before the spartan minimalism
(where alls looks sames)
And the sublime it reaches for descends to
    scald
Detaching retinas not from skull, but sky
The shadows borrow forms from old Ferris
    wheel carts
(And twigboxed faery cartwheels)
Lost in the Enochian walk
Until the shadow grows long in the north
Over nondescript toothpicks of steel
And Chick-fil-A and her siren sisters

Shrink to little more than bioluminescent
lights
In the abyss

Country Gold

You would think the golden lightsaber dawn
That cuts bullion from the foundry axon
Would stay cordoned off in countryside.
You would think the great gold brick from
    outside
Piercing the pane as if all sunlight came
Filled in a piping bag, icing aflame
Through the parallelogram tip, squeezed in
To decorate your bed's sheet cake. Seized him,
Your son, from above, marionette net
So many points of light pulling; jet set
Whips of hair, soft passive smiles, the saccades
—
Lifted. Not Everglades but ever glades,
These things you seek in Florida, the Rockies.
This is no ranch house, no Florida lobbies,
No morning cabin or golden houred wheat.
This, the better printing sister of Fleet
Street. Demon barbers nocturnal napping,
Stereotypes of Brooklyn — kidnapping
And death and porn — hibernate from the
    hoar:
Mount Washington sets minus 104
Wind chill record. Ghosts of boilers flee day

While monogram rings my Azikiwe —
Primum president, first name means "my dad
Is alive," a distinction to be had,
anteindependent Nigerian,
One I do not share, but care's virion
Minds I mind that mine does and will —
    the gold
The watching eye of a floor mirror holds
Now, painting yellow passing dotted lines
Big enough for planes on parquet confines.

Two starlings sit atop the Friedrich metal
Wearing cosmicloaks, their feet tea kettles
Rattling, a chirp like lions roaring
Towards a cave that echos back, exploring
Other acoustic hollows. They watch us
Hidden in our Brooklyn hollow, trochus
Holding what the sun gifted morrow
What was countryside (to rural sorrow).

Not All Leviathans

I find myself subumbrella
Pinkish mesogloan
The cnidarian caught me —
Caught us all —
And it did not sting
But woke

For I alone gaze up in its purple bell
To see beyond my double hung
(And its six story brick implied)
Caught whilst dreamers dream
Of pink and purple things

Speaking of it here spooks it
And our good old pigeon dawn returns
mere lessdark
Mirrorless dirk

But I knew —
And you know —
The Man of War in the present state of having
come in peace
Pluperfect purple
At 6:30 AM in Brooklyn
has left, early, to make his appointment
With some abyssal gigantism

When you're finished with fellow Leviathans,
Eld Friend,
Come meet me here at dusk, once more,
please.

I would like to show my wife your
Blushing green fluorescent protein
What chromophore, Brooklyn dawn,
What deathwatch, coral
What unfallen angel
bleached grey

Defend us in battle.

Handicap Accessible Dreams

Having a kid in New York
Is being handicapped
According to the doors.

The handicapped thrive here
If you know where to go.

You stay here long enough the city will
    kneecap you
And take your hearing
And pocket change.
I know one dying old Brooklyner
Whose hearing aid shattered to pocket
    change.
They excavated his ear,
A basement on which they'd erect
new technocracies.

It is the cost of growing up into a deep rooted
New Yorker, of *insisting* on dreaming in The
City That Never Sleeps
If you can make dreams here sleepless, you can
make them anywhere.
Dream until it becomes *this city's* reality.

Make it here
When you can
Have kids, plant gardens
Lose your hearing
Let them beat and spend the ever living road
tar out of you
Pre-school tuition after pre-school tuition
Grow gloriously handicapped:
Dream.

Having a kid in New York
Is Being. Handy. No Kapp.
According to the tours.

Retirement Plan

My love, when we are old
We, together, must open
A detective agency.

Other couples opt for vineyards,
For summer sands and smaller climbs
And climes.
And clams.
And claims.
And crimes (the committers, the committed).
And chimes.
And tetracyclines.

Not us.

No, no.

Retirement prisons and vacation factories.
I'm sorry, please — please — excuse me,

"Cruises."

Not you and not me,
no ma'am.

You and I shall rain-soaked
Gum-shod and becaned
Seek out them killers and them thiefs and
    yonder philanderers.
Two old farts dressed up
As two young jazz things
Tickling the secrets of the world loose from
    dark ACE Hotels
And begging the beggars to surrender their
    secrets
And sipping our spirits forth from bliss at
    Smalls
And kayaking the Hudson, dragging for
    bodies

Until, at last, we emerge
Dead long past DNR
Letting sons and grandsons deal with our
    nonextant estate
Until a little nurse notices

The answers to the riddles of the earth there
    in our rigor mortis grips
Phone numbers in frozen knuckles
Our other bones twined.

It's that
or pinochle.

I say we sleuth becatheterèd. We can. We can.
Wee, wee can on the weekend
— an elder's second birthday balloon —

With you.

City Dawn #2

The black bars of the plastic frosted piece
From the center of wedding tables see:
This too is country — a hexagonal
Ray, six splayed hands gone all diagonal —
Hanging foreground stencil black fore the
  wash:

Someone has dragged a translunary brush
Across a wet and mostly blue Monet
With bits of amber, indigo, and grey,
Two white gold streams of what had been a
  plane
And only faintest hint on the day
Of the tippy top of a roof A/C.
Oh, and look: the skeleton of a tree.
Tell me: is the sky the beauty or shade?
The haunting finger print of winter's blade
Or the now-moltening pot of cloud bank
Long Island proffers for urbans to thank?

Perhaps they see other sides of solstice,
But one is darkest day; other? Christmas.

The sky affirms by glowing gold the sleet,
"Miracles happen on 34th street."

The Carpenter's Sons

In St. Joes in The Village
Through frankincense sillage
In stained glass a scene is arrayed:

To father, the carpenter,
Legs in full *arpenter*
The Christ child holds out what he played:

(It isn't a hammer,
A bokken, coat hanger,
Wood trinket for memory loss)

He proffers his father
For hope and not pother
The plaything he built: it's his cross.

Light on Pulp

There is a point
where light on pulp
means more than words on page
where the skimming sieve
of morning sun
cleans up the groundwood
the oakendown underbrush
of Amazon's cardboard
till it turns to fresh sheared wool
so thin and clean you could write on it
if you wanted some glad morning

What Summer Costs

Fires Lit
In every window
Of black brick against the blue

Gold frame sits
With orange fresco
Washing every frame to true

Lovers eyes have seen the light
Windows turned from holes to plates
Of proffered treasure, mirrored flight
Squares of summer in the frosts
Squares of what the summer costs:

Purple snowfilled sewer grates

North Wind

The North Wind doesn't howl so much as whistle low and steadily, like something moving along its set track, something spinning in whirling dervish prayers, something enchanting the wine glasses to hum — it turns the whole house into a baritone flute or recorder, one long note in a four story slide whistle that rings on for hours and hours and hours and—

Good morning, North Wind, I see my house as you see her now:

One more church organ hidden among Greater Greenwood's freshly planted urban trees. Thanks for evensong.

she...

Leaves.

Fowlers

What largemouth bass
May eat has airborne
Taken itself in flight
Flight. Yes, you see,

There's a dragon
Fly in the sky
Above the pond
In Greenwood Cemetery

A passerine
Don't ask me which kind,
We will be stuck here for...
Fine! Perhaps it's

A rockfowl, cardinal,
Drone or fantail,
Vanga or warbler,

Nicator, lark

Some old world flycatcher
(I mean that both ways)—
Passes by, old flyer,
Diving through air

To waters where it landed
Gobbles the grub.
And the largemouth, pissed
At the aerial defrauding of what
Earth dragon
Belonged to his deep,
Swallows the sparrow
Instead
And also gets the grub.

Longaevi

Seven male cardinals watch
The wedding party of chickadees
As the blue barrel
Bearlike moves
To eat seed too —
My son.

Perhaps some angels never guard
Some demons never tempt
Longlaevi look on
As we fumble through the termite-riddled
dark —
Turbscorling wet pulp;
Castscat their councils —
So much flapping from their fleeing we ig-
nore, mea culpa,
Fumbling for a feather and a sunflower en
utero.

Alchemy

Magnesium was cast into a pretty coin
And thrown into the evening sky
And blushed with all the heat of summer loin
When sunlight snuck inside it, caught his eye:

The flame of morning sparked the little coin
And white and hot she burned to bring the
waves
And when they came she smoked on sput-
tered bed
And now we're double blind here in the dark.

The Wind Moves like an Echo

"Lance," he calls. Not me, he.
Is it really Narcissism when I move
As primum mobile moves
At the song of my name?
I don't go looking for it,
Diving,
Don't project myself out there
Expecting...

So it comes as a surprise
When I see eyes in everything
Staring back at my selves
That speaks and spells:
The lanceflower calls me,
As do all ants in plants
In all of the lands I inhabit, bespeared.
I hear a Nancy speak of refinancing. Laughs.
    Relapse.
Experience chance meetings in the right cir-
    cumstance
In France. With a lynx for my familiar

in the lancts where my noveliar characters
relax.
But the trance dance grants askance glance.

I turn. "Who me?"
The stranger always shakes their head *no*.
But the God in them and the rest?

He calls to me from everything.
Even when I do not want —
did not dare to expect —
To be *seen*

What a terrible thing to be watched.
What beautiful when by a friend.
"Lance. Lance."
"I heard it, Mpampa. What do I do?"
"Next time he does it —
if it wakes you — say:
'Speak, Lord,
for your servant is listening.'"
"Okay." So later:
"Speak. Speak. Speak. Speak. Speak."

"Lance," he calls. Not me, he.
Is it really Narcissism when I move
As primum mobile moves
At the song of my name?
I don't go looking for it,

Diving,
Don't project myself out there
Expecting...

So it comes as a surprise
When I see eyes in everything
Staring back at my selves
That speaks and spells:
Ten thousand plays Is.

A Note I Left on Grandpa's Broken Pocketwatch

You're worth dying for
worth living for
worth giving, sleeping, waking for
worth crying for
worth lying for
though mostly worth truth-scrying for
worth buying for
worth massive debt
worth risking every bayonet
worth kicking ass and taking for
worth giving life and striving for
worth getting out of all that debt
worth working till we break a sweat
worth stopping till we get our get
worth any timepiece broken over
any worthy love of mine
that took your place
for a time.

A Translation for English Readers of Elon's Tweets

Oh Heavenly Sharts you fill up my hearts
For I'm an abyssal squid.
For shits nor for farts, but your heavenly
sharts
I'd wager a takeover bid.

I'm leveraging shares of my rocketry firm
(since all that has now gone kaboom)
To make heavenly sounds on no more than
the grounds
of the John by the family room.

I, eldritch, once was, 'fore relations called:
"Cuz!
we require a song of the sound
of not shit or a fart, but the cold beating heart
Of the Heavenly Sharts we have found!"

Well a trumpet from rumpets taste better than
crumpets
they bake by latrines in the war.
And a squirt up the shirt from the dairy
yogurt
leaves a mark on the grocery store.

So I set out, a squid, just to settle the bid
so the banks won't foreclose on my engines.
I typically hide my Lovecraftian side
a Cthuluan non-intervention.

It started on Twitter, I took there a shitter,
it spread first to cars then a Doge
And now all the country is shitting and
farting
addicted to our self-reproach.

Cloth-of-Gold

The coffin's skuh-runk
over the axial dark cask rolls that will haul dad,
opening a red curtain,
and the horde of whos in kitchy covered necks
    are inspecting
like condors who crave in the Andes—
corpulant, strange, nosy.
It's dad's Speech Day: these are the fools
showing "respect" on paper and the FM,
pulp of my charged chat swishing dad's Red-
    neck Scarf,
lips of my aunt taut winding under crow's
    feet,
blushing painted on shameless hard lines
like a cosplay rush job of a Sister Who Cared.
Across these watchers, this son shouts loud
    the words of the other son,
preaching a film: father's slow death (days
and then some months without these visitors
now catching up on lost visiting hours).
When his oak goes down under the grave
all these millionaires will wake my pauper
(unintended necromancy)

now I understand why some would eat the
rich.
So here my voice surges, Speaking for the
Dead:
Christian Church, Union, the Pharmacy
Monopoly
old high schoolers, mimicking their scripts of
gossip—
*I loved Steve . . . He caught that murderer that
escaped . . . Did you know he fished pro?*
The morning is fresh on the slick stones,
putrid in the parlor, the heat of the hate
aiming at a son who sees, preaching:
each line leaks out like a hid car's
secret in cracks in the cushions, rusting down,
exposing bones.
The strata of flesh cures and stacks on other
corpses
fat and gristle sloshing high
till centennial parades harbor the old hush-
hush;
spines curve under weight of town's pros-
perous exposé-to-be.
In the idle hearse, *Are you okay?*
asks the mortician who was my father's best
friend,
who just debriefed with me pulling father's
brains out father's nose;
outside go those who wouldn't touch dad.
Across the street from us, for years,
my uncle dragon prowled the Elks
(where dad and friends ate mythic buffalo)
sucking father dry
by pulling father's brains out father's nose
thinking it cloth-of-gold for weaving small
town propoganda garments.

Dad's mind was cloth of gold, but not for un-
cle's hoard.
My new uncle mortician drives us
and my father's illegal Dominican fiancée
To the grave where I will read her Pablo
Naruta in Spanish:
Florida.
My uncle thinks I mean his mobster state.
But she and I and dad's mortician know:
I feel despair for all the quiet folk
I've been nice to
knowing niceties
is how a dragon justifies a Long Lead murder,
And so I speak and spell before
We toss in our flaming *floridas.*

Greenwich: Mean

Before Frost came to time his light
The Time once ticked itself unwound
And locked in sea storm — port and right —
Without a mean, they ran aground.

The papers told him how he'd failed
To murder meter, ships and secs.
Arrhythmic states rejected — wailed
His rock and roll that wasn't sex.

Yet here in Greenwich John H. learned
To be the keeper of the watch
As here in England Frost would burn
In every publication's notch.

The seamen said that Time was wrong,
Yet Harris knew the wrong was man;
Americans said same of song,

But that's before old Frost began

To tame the verse as John H. tamed
Meridians by gear and latch.
Frost sang a bit of wind's true name
To cage free verse
in a pocketwatch.

$00°00'00''$

Why make so much of fragmentary time
In there or here a phone or St. Joe's bell?
Or train times or sets at Small's or Bowery
    rhyme
When Greenwich lines out in copper aeon's
    well?

Since tick is tock, I guess, not aeons (for now)
    —
Though sages now and then will point from
    rays;
And Greenwich mean extends Forever's day
To merely give Eternity a *how*.

The Park's Quantum Superimposition

Our black-wrought iron fence is rounding
  round we three
— and three playgrounds here —
While London planes are whispering of fear
To come on a Hallow's, noises in the tree
Of when a man was burned upon a bon.
The sidewalks mark an X around the pond.
Visions of towers shine through Roman
  plinths
The scent of rivers — I am seeing both:

I cannot find my way — the labyrinth
Of roads in Greenwich could be fairy grass
The superimposition of this quoth
Shows Me and Me, two parks through
  Looking Glass:
The grit beneath my feet is still a sand
That I could melt
Into *which* old Greenwich roosevelt
From which it's smelt?

The London or the New York Park? Which
land?
For both have paupers buried underneath —
Lamp spark and riot spark
The dead both Gaslamp parks bequeath.
Bilocation occult is out of hand
Yet Greenwich makes one place from two or
three.

In London up above observe a Tory
Who takes a record of the time to ship
Tea goods and riot goods
While stars all fixéd won't be whipped
To vote against the pauper's story,
Unburied by the revenanting woods.

While Washington Square Park is laying wait
For Worker Movements, changing up the
deeds
Both of the "good" and owner's tract.
So London banking is revised by reeds
That paupers picked and dipped in ancient
trees.
And so they delve
To grip their constitution by helve,
Rewrite, and shelve.

Our black-wrought iron fences are blurring at
the seams
— middle men dissolve
Till artisan and his guard are both convolved

To be hung on a wall and not the livestreams;
To be burned in the hearts and not upon
 a bon;
To be drowned in men's love and not in the
 pond;
To be carved of stone and Roman plinths.
And paid for both, which founded Both.

I cannot find my way — the labyrinth
Of roads in Greenwich turns the fairy grass.
The superimposition is now gone.
And us and U.S., two parks, now float as ash
 —
the grit beneath my feet — and now I stand
With what I smelt:
Is there yet a swelling bloody welt
To feed poor arts from punctured svelte?

Amy on the Piers

She's alone. Ice on the fired stone, clearer
Than Amy, sticking.
Someone is getting
Conceived or is a someone — Amy its hearer
    —
She ought leave unto a ball — unconceived
    getting?
Then Amy too is sticking to the pole.

Amy of the Red Hook Frostbitten sang
    all morn
Restoring. Muse of fewer soles
Whose none are hearing,
Leave her alone with piers and dark,
Still waters. Grace rises
Of infantile.

Here is a birth ward.

Contract-y gal to conceive sweet batter
Born out & hears in the ice & doubles down.
How every soul there is afraid of the kids.
Hear on, Heaven's dancer,
For a tap-tap breath.

Sounds sound out from sound boats sounding sounds

The sailor's exchanging a sound for a sound
Next to the bow of the Red Hook fiddler;
Yet yonder in ship hulls gone to ground
His soundings expose our corporate diddlers:

Her moorings are tucked — illegal ties —
Whenever he's coming ashore for shrimp
And now he is munching them synchronized:
Their harmony louder than Colonel blimp.

Still I feel from my Hinnomian ferry
If all in our Valleys know fire from fire?
For here in progressions conserve contraries:
Aelion Sails keep on weeping the Lyre.

A Ghost Story

Your goal I saw while crossing
Manhattan Bridge overpass —
Red jersey, mown grass, blown net —
Through holes in the D train's tracks.

Then you and I were ruptured.
Torn from one another's skies.
Still, Reader, I cheer; say, "hi."

Papa: if you're up there still,
Ride a rail over my words
Watch me score this poem, please
Knowing ***you're*** watching ***them*** feel
What I feel as you feel what I feel —
That you feel them —

chills the reader.

Green Thumb

Most days I wake up missing you.
And most days I think most folks do too
For their you.
How anything lives or moves or breathes
This broken down inside
Baffles me — that British film in 1973 —
must be some other source keeping us going.
It seems we're rather good at stopping fore we
start.
Yet it's spring...

I should be planting things, I should be
sowing oaks.
I should be grafting and taking cuttings
— truly taking
Stealing shoots
Smuggling a biodiversity of climes into some-
where mine
Planting the whole planet in the backyard
Caper green.

It's the only thing I have trouble planting,
plants.
I wish I had a hedge labyrinth.
Your tomatoes were fifteen feet tall.
I don't ever need to exaggerate: you
And I know it's true. That's enough.

I wake up the next day having lost the thread
Then the memory of having not lost the
thread yesterday
Again, is waking up missing you
And the parts of you
On the whole, most days most folks do.
Your green thumb...
Oh had that part saved the whole.

Tonitrum

Two Taiwanese women dressed for Wimbledon terrorize a shredded shuttlecock, trying to force the other to fail. But the stormfront of a rainbomb threatens plastic funnel wings with wet.

It's also that children have turned on twenty sprinklers over pavement replaced with broken water balloons tinted radioactive. And noise: the man in the leafblower corralling the choking hazards, rubberized shreds of petroleum.

Spider lightning licks green boughs. The light disturbs the women: neither remembers who lost the cock as headfirst it gongs the drummetal tables. They laugh at one another, me, kids.

Thunder follows. Both lose to the stampede.

The Structure of the Transcendent

Before the brothers in the Catskills
Put their Love to song
They met in New York, Beverly Hills
To put to right the wrong

Before the Thomists of the foothills
Sang aloud the right
They only heard the singing
Of the paupers in the night:

Age beyond age in straw huts
The friars of Francis came
To meet the man who's Of the Lord
— a practical Spaniard with too much sword;
Italian bright as a Frankish gourd —
As a crowd who sought The Name.

For the love of Dominic proffered

Provisions they'd prepared;
While the love of Francis bothered
The poor till lords they were declared.

For Dominic towered on footmark
Before, like a dog, he'd leap.
While Francis, catlike, leapt in the dark
To the cry of the loon and the song of the lark
Till colossus, Dominic, shouted, "HARK!"
Fore Frank would land on his feet.

And Dom had brought his vittles
For every vowing monk
But the countryside came to feed the friars —
Kings and merchants hiked through the briars
And the birds with their berries; bread from
  the squires;
And wine on the back of the skunk.

The peasants carted wine and game
The nobles dug out their carts.
The reckless faith of God was ordered
Hours of prayer and abby bordered
But the faith in God has a true disorder:
Faith in all new mens's hearts.

From there old Francis went crusading
Not with sword or horse
But with the mind of man on God,

The canticle of Sun and Sod,
And the hope of beauty making odd
The reason of stars in their course.

And Dominic nodded agreement
And cheerfully cheered him on:
"Tis better to win persuading men
Enlightening dark and healing sin.
Prosecute, don't persecute wins —
By love our great world spins on."

It was taken up by Thomas
Old Bonaventure's friend
Who cited Muslims, Jews, and Greeks
And spoke in the tongues that Jesus speaks
And hopes for a time when war will cease
When the martyrs will descend.

For the old Halensis Summa
On which Thom built his book
Says Beauty's the form of all transcendent,
Structure, fundament, truth resplendent,
All desire's last ascendant
The tryst of bread and book.

Behold the Millennial as He Bikes Behind the Bus

High on leaded gas and Red Dye 40
The Boomer joins Congress as a Tory
And argues Portage Glacier observation
Decks "have not closed from global
cremation"
That forced Portage Glacier to hide from
view;
Argues it's not due to junk he hopes you
Use daily:
vitamin capsules (seem oiled),
Bicycle tires —bleed black when burned or
boiled —
Mops stink when melted, fake wool when
felted,
Lectric blankets turned dad's shed to smelted
Slag, two stories of tin, like crayon molds
That too are formed from Texan blackened
gold,
Dyes, fishing flys, car enamel, golf bags,
Hair curlers (melting), paint rollers (smelting),
Sweaters and slacks — polyester felting
All these things he worships come from
petrol.
Hiding beneath his plastic bedroll.

Bright eyed, choose, what Boomers could've
 avoided:
Look in the mirror, leave unexploited
A part of any particular thing
Left better in the ground than on a ring.

Millennial: "I'll bike behind the bus."

The Boomer writes exposés on how thus
Their dumbass will die from petrol fumage
(Stroking: himself, Route 66 plumage)
And never stops to think we all could lay
Our bodies on the altar of today
So tomorrow's kids might not grow up high
On leaded gas and on Red 40 dye.

Radiator Caesarian

They brought in the sound of my grandfather's woodshop
Right where I was typing.
The wind of their sawing chased dust bunnies airborne —
The first and last flights of the low castes of Valkyrie.
Valves needed mending.
The waterline had invaded the bookshelves,
Waiting for reading, for ruining works.

They cut it whilst I drafted.
And the radiator had an ocean in it.
And did more damage than over the months it had done in seconds.
"toallas! toallas!"
So I grabbed my buddy's towels.
A five gallon bucket we'd been using for laundry, recycling.
"mas pequeño."
So I grabbed a stainless steel mixing bowl, the one for the eggs.

There's jazz playing. Jon Batiste.
I make them coffee, pecans, Pockys
(Which are basically both with sugar).

On the grinding goes. I will not be revising.

Body count:
5 ruined books.
2 ruined bookshelves.
10 feet of ruined parquette floor.
1 castrated radiator.
No.
Rather, 1 radiator that, as with my bride, has
    had seven layers of tissue cut through her
    womb to birth the child which is the only
    cure for an infected placenta
A world that gave her 150 doctors appoint-
    ments believing birth some disease to cure
Only to realize, later, their diseased thought,
    since birth was the only cure
3rd revision on the novel interrupted. Again.

But hey, this poem was born
from that clattering racket of winter heat.
Childbirth's weird.

The Worldmaker

Six died in dustdown of I-55,
Thirty-seven hospitalized alive,
Seventy-two vehicles caught in storm
that seemed spewed forth in the wake of
a worm
from Dune. In Illinois, there lived a boy
named Lance, who found — a pen — his fa-
vorite toy
and wrote of a land of orchard honey
and whitetail and coal and Easter bunnies,
the green and red and July blueberries
he'd heard tale of and seen. Adversaries
came and robbed the forrest clean of ichors
from the veins of the Riverland, strikers
stopped it not. Fed the blood of Shawnee gods
— machina ex deo — to heat our sods
until they all amalgamate with air.
It turned our once habitable affair
into a neither-breath-nor-sowing place.
There was a dustbowl by farmer's disgrace,
but this one isn't on them. It's on us.
How many tsunamis will "It's not fuss,
but death" take for us to admit? Look now:
the very dirt is killing sacred cows.

The Orienteer

He is out of self-induced traffic
    And speeding

He is charging by the mile
    But hopefully not the kilometer

He stops before the monolith of a line painter's truck
    Before the square where once a year parades Macy's

He is shouting, "Yo!" At that driver
    That driver is shrugging, steaming white

He is back in self-induced traffic
    And speeding and not. And then again, out and speeding.

"Where is Madison Square Garden?"

"That was it. This is the shop. That was— stop. Take my money, for the love of God. For the love of God stop, stop, open the damn door and stop, what are you, *Taxi Driver*?"

"Why, yes, sir, thank you, sir, good day to you, sir, and leave five stars for my quick trip."

"I will never. I need a donut."

Storyweavers

The limners came laughing at my work.
For all my scrivening, scraps of life
Sat stoic — a stillicide
Of tea ran off the tip of my desk
After having altered inks.
Potion or not — ink or the pulp
Of Camellia's spent mashed leavings —
Nothing has woken the words I penned.
The limners asked me to let them try.
I shrugged and sucked the spit from my pipe
And spat it to land in the lake of spittoon.

Word-paintings and paint-summons
Danced from their tongues. The dazzled
strands
Attached to their stylets. Tied off and bright,
Motley and glowing, they painted the magic
Of what I had meant. Whence arcane?
Whither its end? Even the rainbow:
Page sucking and starting a new
Way of telling the tale I wanted.
I saw before my face a sign:

Animals of mind I'd made alive;
Gold trinkets with virtue and truth;
Stylets on stylets with the great strengths
Of the many makers of the megacosm;
Sundry monsters; Seven lights;
The archive of the redemptive clockwork,
deemed.

I looked at the limners and loved them,
For they manifested what my manuscripts
Had passed beyond in silence yonder.

Then they left my office, light of the cloaks
Of each of them easing to an early dusk
As a murmuration of starlings,
Each sable feathered cloak a womb of worlds.
And to my dust I do return.
But even in the spire of my ache-lonely
Castle in the quagmire, I miss their quirks,
Their glamorous smirks, their glowing flashes.
Little lingers in my eyes but the light
I memorized when they made light
Of my work and words and wondrous
dreams.

Bookish Prison

I built myself a bookish prison
All around my bookish desk
And wondered if by bookish labor
I'd be laid to bookish rest.

Each stalagmite dripping skyward
Grew as thoughts congealed on each,
Growing — tasks of essays drafting —
Grasping far beyond my reach.

William Conches said we're dwarven
Seers on a giant's back,
Seeing further not by stature,
But cause giants penned our lack.

This is only true for readers.
Seldom does the world default
To seeing further than the giants:

Shatters what was once gestalt.

Yet by climbing up these drippings
In this cavern cell of books,
First by scrapes and then by slippings
I will find a place to look:

See there from my bookish prison
To tomorrow's bookish desk:
In your eyes, by bookish labor,
You shall read my bookish rest.

Teamhair

They named you a mansion
In Gone with the Wind
That Scarlett had named from
The Mount of the Kings
And I'm full of my sin
And I'm empty of things
But you are the hill that I've
Died on, Tara,
You are the hill I'll die on, Tara
Making a sinner a king.

A Service

My buddy was a special forces gun
And thinks there's knowing, then there's
    knowing still.
That one will come from bones, another life
And poets of The Life are better ones.

There is a third, of course, the man who lives
Ten thousand lives by reading book on book
Librarious living, richer in pain
A man like this could see, could put to pen:

The hidden solid ghost my gun awoke
Would not recant, would not recall when asked.
Once summoned by a tiny little switch.
It reft the air, it shook the chests of us.
The movement was a woodland curious —
A chipmunk, squirrel, mole, or easter hare —
I flinched and called my demon to the air
To drive a roofing nail into the vase
That held the brain of such a little boy.

How earlier he'd given me a toy
That gave libations — candy — one by one
And taught me: still the civil can be found.
The wild is not without, it is within.
The thing that windchime physics loves,
So many slender rods of music
Falling everywhere.

This time in clanged cacophony
And loose with fishing wire you see
A Cracker Jack encircle dripping gore
From a fighter that had given me something.

This did not happen.
Now it did, you see.
And so my pacifism suiteth me.
Never will I "thank you for your service,"
But I will sit and listen, say, "I'm so
So sorry all this happened to your soul,
So here is mine in trade."

Sanderson said that you can't rhyme with bulb

Sanderson said that you can't rhyme with
    bulb —
Rhyming in lexicons often agree.
Neither considered the mulberry tree,
the bulbil of leaf axils, deeper medula's
bulbar paralysis (my Vegas nerve):
the verve of the mid-word dueling rhyme
is better than slanting on pulp bulbously.

My toddler in the cemetary

Look, Pap, the fishies.
Look, Papa, I touched dem.
Pap. Look, Papa, dey nibbling my toes.
Dey won't eat me, it's okay, Pap. Dem big
ones only eat dead fings. My toes is live.
Look, Papa, blue heron. He gone catch dem.
He eat live things. He go so so slow. So so
sneaky.
Just fishies, it's okay, not my toes. He eat just
fishies.
Look, Papa, I found a button. It on da
ground.
Look, Papa, I found confetti. Where it from?
Was it a wedding? Look, I unroll it. Look
the wind take it. Look. Look at it in the
wind. It gone touch de wildflowers. It's
okay. It's okay Papa, the rain melt it. It
basically toilet paper. It melt. It's okay, it
turn to Greenwood Cemetery someday.
Look, Papa, a big old stick. Is it a Bilbo day or
a Gandalf day?
Look, Papa, those people dead. That boy's
named Arthur too, see the stone?

A.R.T.H.U.R. Arthur! Like me. Was he happy? The dead little boy?
Look. Look, now.
Are you sad Pap? Why you sad? It's okay. It's okay, Papa, I'm here.
I'm still here papa with the fishies, with you.
See? My toes is live.
Dey won't eat me, it's okay.
Look, Papa. Was it a wedding? He eat live things. Is it a Gandalf third day?

Normal Mornings

I am weird enough to judge my days by
    normal mornings
Whether I rise at ten to five, showered quick
Whether I beat the birds with my own
    morning noise
Glanced in my wordcount fever to see the
    pane's
Dawn-and-bough-silhouette book cover
Writing of murder or lying or greed
Praying I get it right.
Wait, wait. Not a murder, I mean,
Not get a murder right, not pull it off,
    wait, I—

Today, though, others have beaten me
9th avenue is borderland Hasidic
And the dawnsong of Passover echoes
Over Brooklyn bricks needing pointed
So that my firstborn son's room stops
    molding and plaster stops falling.
The song issues from conservative Jews who
    hate Zionism

Who think Palestine should be a state

They pray a lamb will come
And take the place of their firstborn infants
That the Angel of Death will, for this year, be slaked
And fly its drone wings elsewhere

In the story I'm writing, the young first born black child
Lies beneath a street light, alone, praying until he's
Eaten alive by small town police.
The camera does not cut away. It reads:

You don't expect to end while hearing humans
Eat bits of your hamstrings, biceps, and pectorals,
but here he was. Here he was for a little while longer.
It was only a couple of moments after that they cracked his sternum
and ripped out his heart before him.
And it also wouldn't end, the pain. You don't expect that either.

My son? My little one?

I am weird enough to judge my days by
normal mournings.
Whether I rise. Whether I beat the metal birds
with mourning noise.
Whether, in my word count fever, I see the
pain.
Bough-and-dawn-silhouette book cover
(Sometimes sun brings light, sometimes trees)
Writing of murder or lying or greed
Praying I get it right.
Murder, I mean.
Today I hear the song. I hear it.
I weep.

Overnighters

The professor assigns the deadlines
The absolute last no exception must be graded
grading deadline
I audit
And I audit the beaks in the cherry blossoms
Students haggle dates based on degrees
Singing harmonies with the black man
mowing
Around the neogothic windows of the Duane
Library basement
Our windows are high for us, looking up and
out and bright
Low for him, looking down and in and dark
Those black solderings hold a double meaning
as I've said:
"Stained glass seams."
He could crash in, you know
— I audit, I dream it —
Blades chop up theology table into mulch for
cheery trees
Mono no aware
The absolute last no exception must be graded
incarnating deadline
Is perhaps such a slice of life and theory

Is Christ's humanity particular or universal?
"Both," I audit.
By so many philosophical scents I audit the
grass's screams.
The professor assigns the deadlines
And lifelines at Applebees where he buys us
food and drinks.
I do not miss 3am cosmic horrors on caffeine,
for
Daylight brings me plenty.

The Substack Sonnet

So long to an endless high-school
Reunion. Welcome to new crowds
And readers, midsummer and yule.
Let's propagate the endowed
Poetic. Aren't we now avowed
To spread renown, not fame?
Let's revive, sow, and resurrect
Sehnsucht. Let's recover games
Of innocence long after shame,
stand upon and fish our silver perch,
Paid to herd the public's domain.
Let poetry revive our church.
Let's sub, embody ghostliness,
Fly in concrete's prosiness.

Love Quest

My wife and I
    once slept separately.

Two beds cause
    of her projectile

vomit ten
    days after

our wedding.
    It was the worst

smell. I caught it ringing
    in a steel bowl.

She cried:
    "I feel like we're roommates."

"Oh kiddo,"
    I said,

"No roommate
    would do this."

As the acid hit the bell
    I wondered: well,

at least we arrived early at
    sickness and health.

The gate of the dead

The socialist found a tomato plant
With its vine connecting the fruit
Then call all the fruits their tomato plants
No matter the stem or root.
"Tomatoes: they all are equal," they said
But some of the plants don't care,
They stole bananas, nuts, and bread
And shorn the cornfield's hair.

The New Age shaman found a ghost
And in the teeth of robots
Claimed that spirits are and therefore good
But demons use their brains for food
And seizures they sent to roast them.

The Calvinist found a dead raccoon
And said, "It's destiny."
The atheist agreed with him
Both pointed to a tree:
"Its destiny: to live or die

Is like the dead raccoon."
They said the same of road and care
and mandible and moon
But when they pointed to each other
Neither could agree.
For one was destined for his God,
The other for his trees.

The men and women came for years
Claiming little things escaped
iron fence's spikes,
The oft-ignored estate.

The coon had wandered,
Maters had its body off outside,
Inside the wall of iron spikes
The ghost had hitched a ride,
Inventors liked their progress,
Mayors liked the vow,
But only when it's empty
And only when it's now.

New Yorkers like the simple things
But only when alone
They had no categoried groups
Of simple men and crones.
The cowboy liked the dignity
And freedom of his rights,
But not when they must yield to good,
And to the Just, the Right.

They each found trinkets there outside.
I wandered in the gate
They all went home as darkness fell,
But there inside the light was blinding.
Years did I adjust
And when at last I saw the land
It made me make my trust:

For coons were choosing many paths
And fruits were more than red.
United cornucopia,
But still unique, not dead.
The ghosts were good because they knew
That demons do exist
And I had not the memory
To keep track of the list
Of all that was inside the gates.
So curious, I bloomed.
For everything was tempered —
Warp by weft upon the loom
The story of existence
Of the tale of wind and bliss:
It was ordered, fame and formal garden
— wood that none had missed.
I would never delve the depth of it
And never walk its bounds
For each idea was tempered
By the others's ends and grounds.

In the morn I threw the gate
To let the others in

But they called it scary, lame, and old
And called the truth a sin.

I left portcullis open,
But wandered back inside
To see how fruit depends on soil,
How raccoons need the fruit tree's toil,
How hosts were once like coons (when
    boiled)
Man to soul and skin.

To Dr. Cirilla — On Writing Poems Blind to One's Talent

It is sane to pen the poems you alone can
write
for minds are of one mind to keep what a man
has writ aright,
like the Pensieve knows how a moment that
trauma'd you as the sea
seen right: is still and stoic, deep roots, trunk,
and tree —
for a poem lets our fingers run along whatever
moves
that we might touch an encounter and know
true its many old grooves.
It is sane to just deposit in the Pensieve, tell
of the moments you're alone keeping (their
magical spell).
By the hiding of thoughts you're storing in
gold rings
(like the copperminds of Sazed) the quick-
silver (its molten wings)
of the endless shifting wonder of your en-
chanted Faerie Land
Where holiday magic and holy songs oft go
hand in hand.

Poems and stories swirl in all as nostalgic,
flashing storms
That hope to live and have much matter but
cannot find their forms.
You wish you could be a mind as Coleridge,
but he had writer's block:
No grading would have come into his old Pen-
sieve, nor your English professor's clock.
He could not write one of the poems you
wish that you could write
Nor see the swirling in the Pensieve that
wracks thy brain at night.
I need not see anything: no resume nor skill.
I only know thy silver heart shalt not thy Pen-
sieve kill.
So deposit poems and stories, and they will be
very good:
for the mind of them in the bowl is sane re-
membering what it should.

The bird and The day

He digs in the play doh
    With infant fingernail clippers
    "Digging. Digging. Dig dig dig dig digging."
    He says.

The starlings are stealing the nests
    Of other angels who have fallen
    While others merely steal from angels

You can have both:
    The creation,
    The creative theft.

He throws the play doh wallward, frustrated.

Originality and derivation
    Can both either help or hurt.
    It all depends on the bird and the day.

Petal Wings

Pink petals rain
After the songbird's call
And huge shadow of wings cross my toes

I know not what bird.
I know birds. I have never heard this song
    before.
Nor did the shape of wings feel familiar —
What size, what span, what spread —

There! It moved again. See?
Blossoms mark its wake,
But not water.
Only this eldritch sky.

If creatures of pure mind
Disembodied exist
I would expect a fearsome song.
I would expect some foreign wingspan.
I would expect a trail of pink silks;

Petals tailing a wedding gondola.

Think what you will.

On my 38th birthday I *still know* I met an
angel
Underneath two ancient cherry trees.

Mono No Aware

Pink carpet
Soft as tissue
Thick as already snowfall

A two body system
Thousands of pink giants
Shedding their light
In collisional cascading
A torrential orbit of Kessler syndrome
Blossoms hitting blossoms shedding corolla
Beautiful space debris
Seeding other solar systems
Deep in Greenwood's bays

These are the two oldest
Cherry trees I have ever known
In person or grown
Somewhere else
Online

They say plant pears for your heirs
But I am glad
The Fairbanks family whose proto-erection
Of a gravestone plinth
Planted these
for me.

I'll let it rain pink light upon my face awhile in
this high wind
Tornadic sakura
物の哀れ
Lacrimae rerum
And wonder if life isn't gratuitous sunrises
Tickling my cheek's tears
Cast from the open palm of some long dead
saint

Homeland Generation

I once dug out a turd, a perfect sphere,
From out a sixteen-year-old's ass and cheeks.
It rolled as if a shooter marble tracked
By twinning wineskins: apathy and fear.
The nurse who oversaw my rooms those weeks,
She said, "I'll take no shit, where is his dad?"
The teen'd snapped his ankle — "Robes off. Here." —
— but still could squat. His case, it wasn't bleak.
Both child and father Janie took to task
As I beheld the turd I'd snatched in hand:

"When dads like you don't make him wipe his ass
His generation fears rock, stock, and glass."
She turned, "Oh Lance, I love your mercy, grit.
From now on let kids figure out their shit."

WHAT IF POETS

what if poets
grew from the grease
mechanics secrete
and farmers eat
and little boy blues all lost and confused
pick from the girls to eat?

what if the companies
shut all their mouths
so only the sounds of
copywrit coffee grounds
early one morning would bleat?

we likely would cease
to vote in the men
whose BEST SMARTEST GOODEREST
canned response can
effect nothing of substance
when the one dying man
is the millionth to choke in the street.

Until I moved to Brooklyn

Until I moved to Brooklyn
    The water was as Cana.
    "I cannot come to your birthday party
    Cause of Rosh Hashana."

Is like if from my region
    In Southern Illinoisky
    "I cannot come to your birthday party
    Cause Casimir Pulaski."

Ode to a Windfucker

When Proto-Indo-European men
Thought up a word for when they'd strike or
punch
Or stab each other every now and then
(Or thrust with penis, strike with cue and
such)
The word they found's now Swedish for
"to fire
From work" and Dutch for "breed amok."
Infer by speaking, jumping double dutch
Entendre leaves you thunderstruck
Till names of eagles beg a qualifier:
A kestrel lives whose namesake is "to fuck."

Pondering names with "fuck" inside is hard
As dealing with the "niggard" adjective:
Seeming a slur, though not a greeting card,
It's still far cry from n-word's tragic life.
So goes the lives of kestrels striking wind
Harder and harder, seeming sexual.
To pure, all things are purer. Sitting ducks
to misrepresent

To us what ought be name unsexual:
"They named it well, windfucker: wind it
fucks."

But no! Their fucking is not *fucking* now.
The *fucking* "fuck" we mean is with a cock.
(Apologies for swearing here^ to show
How etymology is like a lock:)
While cocks with talons diving, piercing cow,
Are fucking mice like plucking rice, a hawk.
"To fuck" — not to commit a crasser deed —
Is fucking with the fucking of her strike.
As ass with mules and bitch with lady dogs,
The windfucker's own cock
All amputated off — a eunuch breed —
Could still kick, punch, attack, and root
like hogs
And thus it still be called "It fucks from
wind."

The problem with the words that sound
the same
Is: "Sounds sound out from sound boats
sounding sounds."
And thus four words that share an equal name
Are fucking four new meanings t'wards one
dirt.
The windfucking bird who seems anemophile
—
Recalls to mind an aerial ladder truck —
Anemotupt's the word
Of airstrike birds whose form of yellow bile
Punches, punks, and rubs claw swords.

While crasser minds — apologies — think
  "fucks."

I do not blame the wonderpus for zits.
The fungus beetle did not grow your mold.
Lumpsuckers get not blame for teeth-on-tits.
And fairy armadillos don't steal gold.
Satanic leaf-tailed geckos do not draw
Chalk pentagrams on walls to summon
  ghosts.
So why on earth we'd fuck back striking bird
Whose name should prompt not shame, but
  rather awe:
Windfuckers' name, a lexical signpost—
The ump has called us out: three fucks on
  words.

For Union dues, I say we go on fuck.
And if forgetting, say we've been fucked
  dumb.
For in two places, lightning never fucks.
We fuck a deal, a match, and now snare
  drums.
We're pleased as fuck and roll with sucker
  fucks.
We pack a fuck and fuck above our weight.
Go fuck the clock post-work and ride with the
  fucks.

For to the pure are pure
All words we mean for sure

Like fucks of those bloodsuckers
That punch the old windfuckers:
Yes if mosquitos hold some good,
If woodfuckers can fuck some wood,
If waterfuckers fuck tide higher,
And flamefuckers can fuck with fire,
All keep our blood warm as claws secure
Hot fresh dead mice — WINDFUCKER!

Sympathy

A family of machinists
Is still no cold machine
Neither function nor dysfunction
Is what a family means

A programmer hangout often
Speaks of their broken lines of code
But they are not their if and thens
Society's no mode

My wife, she comes from engineers
Who build our rockets, planes,
And understood that raising kids
Like bombs turn kids to banes.

And Elon Musk invests in firms
That think they're building minds.
But minds assume the tools they use

Will help them see and not abuse,
Projecting sight to blind,
Personifying kinds:
Like buttons (calculations)
Or a ballpoint's bleed (menstration)
Or a stamp (imaginations)
You'd have better luck with worms.

The book has not a memory.
It needs the author's thought
And reader's deep reflection,
Debate of Is and Ought.

The language is a parasite
A symbiotic truth:
Depends on mind and spirit, flesh,
Our words are sown, our words are threshed,
Community and tooth.

So don't back up the river
And do not fight the tide
From mind to machinations
thought still flows
No matter thinks or feels or knows
How love from mind to mind will grow
"Dysfunction's" just our pride—
How does dem neighbors feels inside?

The Postcollonial Dating Scene According to a Haitain

Deep down I delved in New York's grates
To find the sewers chomping:
Their bars smelt... ripe... like moldy tripe.
I met a lady zombie.

"Well you remind me of my ex,
I'm gonna rip your heart out,"
She said and sipped a liquid hex:
Coagulated blood-gout.

She talked of art, ate flesh and chips,
We flirted there for hours.
It shifted to apoca-lips.
I bought her wilting flowers.

I didn't let it escalate,
I wasn't very certain.
For all my friends who came with me

Had turned to mindless carbon.

My buddies paired off, girl and boy.
They took home undead dates.
A week had passed, we reconvened:
Now rots what copulates.

'Fore zombies shown in cinema —
Those postcolonial fiends —
Say less about the folk we hate
And more how ships careened
From English empire to the shores
Of Haiti, land of "Other."
How waves and waves of death and slaves
Are decomposing brothers.

Rotting bodies can't be fought
And neither can a theft
That's pulled on scales of nation-states,
A split, an axen cleft
Divided not by blade or tide,
But scion, tongue, and trade.
The bite infects, for days it hides,
Till native love betrays.

I do not love my zombie girl.
I do not hate her guts.
I understand. She too's infected:
Union Jack or huts?

The summers in Joplin

In summer in Joplin you'll sweat through your poplin
    And want to give beard to your barber.
    While munching on cold cuts you'll learn of the peanuts
    We got from George Washington Carver.

Now Carver was nuts for the lower inputs
    and the fixing of nitrogen farmers.
    So he took all his brains to buy peanuts by trains
    That would ship to George Washington Carver

He then fixed up T.B. by the nut of the pea
    Though the sales of the cure were lackluster.
    When the F.D.A. banned it, old Carver he canned it
    And sold it for hair to have lustre.

Them Neosho summers be hummers and drummers

If you haven't a mill or a harbor.
But tell old Tuskegee, Neosho addressee,
You *know* of George Washington Carver.

They'll send you four starches, four flours, then march ya
Some seventy dyes and wood filler,
Molasses and coffee and old peanut toffy
And sweetened potato painkiller.

Old Carver he sold it and rolled and remold it
To any old fool that would buy
The snakeoil or bake oil he pulled from the clay soil
The grace of the rain from the sky.

See it don't really matter if hero's Mad Hatter
For saints could be pirates on charter.
Just ask old St. Patrick if snake-out-the-hat trick
Did work for George Washington Carver.

For Patrick, he chased all the pirates by grace
'Cross the sea. So they stole up the harbor
That the poor black men gave by the sweat of the slave
And the fathers of Washington Carver.

So old Carver packed manumission in sacks
    For the slaves: half a mercer, half martyr.
    How he got all the gold doesn't matter. It's told
    That he gave it, George Washington Carver.

So when you eat Jiffy or Smuckers or Skippy,
    Just think past your sandwich and further:
    The spread on your bread gave the poor gold from lead
    That the thieves gave George Washington Carver.

Threnody for a Spaniel

She came to us unbidden once
Was strewn about — a stray.
Dumped, she was, by midwest dunces
Out there on the way
Between the four-four interstate
And highway one-sev'n-one.
They left her lonely in the rain,
A canine hit-and-run.

In childhood, how I felt an envy
For the pets I knew.
The dogs and cats and parakeets
Would leave me overdue
For all attention they would get
From friend or kin or foe.
I wanted no young baronet
To steal my minstrel show.

She'd chase my Escort pulling out

Through SUVs and trucks.
I know not how she made her route
Without once getting struck.
Yet still I did ignore the dog
And wall myself inside.
A tiny, lonely, demagogue,
From empathy I'd hide.

For three full weeks I said, "We can't,"
To every whine and bark.
The neighbors came to reenchant
Me: "Hear this meadowlark?"
I said, "I cannot take her in."
They said, "This here's Humane."
They pointed to the next door shop.
I said, "Their way's insane.
They are a kill facility."
They said, "And this beats that?
For three weeks now she's been outdoors."
That's quite the caveat.
So first we fed her in the yard
And tied her to the porch.
But she was cold and disregarded,
"Here's a hut! A torch!"

She needed room to run and so
I bought her then a stake
And leash so long she ran the yard,
As long as python snakes.
We came back from vacation once
And found her nowhere near.
I thought that she'd gone rogue again,
I searched the wood in fear.

But in the back, the warehouse shop
Belonging to the org
Had stolen her. Their agitprop
Was bad as any morgue:
"We know you didn't want her so
We put her in the shed."
"What is this cut? What is this scar?"
I asked, "Why's she half-dead?"

And back and forth through Valentines
We argued with those two
Until we got our doggy back
And put her in our zoo:
We'd made a doghouse hind the fence
"I let thee runneth free."
But then it got too cold and thence
She turned inside, you see.

We penned her in the washer room.
She barked at us each night.
And so we moved the gate and broom
Into the kitchen light.
But then she barked and so we let her
Roam square footage free.
Except our own door would prevent her
From the bedroom, see.

But she was then a lonely pup
Not yet e'en six months young.

And every night she'd wake us up —
How sad the songs she sung.
We hemmed, we hawed past New Year's Day,
She sang her elegy.
That's how the spaniel got her way,
Her mattress tenantry.

"What should we name her?" Tara asked.
I said, "I've been a fool —
As bad as narcissists unmasked,
Afraid of barks and drool.
And yet her whining won my heart
In pouring rain, and so:
I say we make the contrast hard
And name our dog Echo."

We took her on the road to mountains,
Switchback river vales.
She rode the trains, the ferry fountains,
Subways, streets, and trails.
We flew her on our business trips
And every time they said,
"We didn't know you had a dog!
She's quiet as the dead!"

They were not wrong, for tonce she tried
To take her doggy life.
Oh that she lived and had not died
Is glory to my wife:
For early on she ate a puck

Of poison in the woods
Of Ozark Mountain countryside
So far from vet or goods.

We had but forty minutes left
To make our thirty drive
And so I gunned it to the vet
To keep my girl alive.
A purgative and charcoal came —
We got the poison up.
I had adopted wild, untame,
This lion-hearted pup.

Then back to Ozark mountains climbed
And huckleberry picked.
She sniffed the lignin, lapped my typing,
Barked her benedict.
To Hillspeak once in storms we drove
A borrowed minivan.
Had she not barked before the mudslide
Come would fall of man.

And once she quaffed a pan of trub
I'd brewed into a beer,
Which rose by two degrees temp up
Each minute. So the fear
Again would make me leave a party
Driving quick as quail:
Flushed her blood of spent hops hardy,
Doctor didn't fail.

Then afterwards I brewed more beer
And made some cider, wine.
She cheered me to move past my fear
My little constantine.
Then moved to Brooklyn on the pavement
Bagels she would find,
Which flared her up, her carb enslavement,
Whole loaf or in rind.

We purged more poisons, fixed more ailments
Cooking chicken, rice.
And once upon a time her gall
Would threaten paradise.
But surgery and meds restored her
To her playful years
Until she got quite sick again,
Calling up arears.

The doctor asked, "When she is sick
How do you keep her fed?"
"We feed her chicken and some rice
And keep her still," I said.
We listed symptoms. "She's allergic
To the chicken meat."
Which they had put inside her meds
So each she'd want to eat.

Back when we got her, our old house

Was there on Emperor.
Quite near to Eaglewood it sat,
A cross adventurer.
But near them both was Echo Valley,
Prophesied in black.
And south of that, an omen, rally,
Easter Road in back.

Yet now in New York we have lived
For longer than in woods.
She's lived the life our mothers missed
And shared in all our goods.
But last night something happened deep
Inside our puppy's brain.
It forced her body right in sleep,
She turned and turned in pain:

Barrel roll by barrel roll she
Tried to chase her ear.
Dogfights work with biplanes, bees,
But not to oversteer.
A tumor, then, and far too late
For Cockers last but twelve.
For sixteen years she's served us, great:
What heights and depths she delved.

She came to us unbidden once
Was strewn about — a stray.
Dumped, she was, by midwest dunces
Out there on the way.

Now with toxins they have killed her
In my arms today.
She isn't shaking, isn't willed,
And isn't in the way.

She came to us unbidden once
Was strewn about — a stray.
Dumped, she was, by midwest dunces
Out there on the way.
We can't afford a burial
In Greenwood by The Greats.
Nor burn her ashes aerial —
Alone or with her mates.

But I cannot afford cremation
How to tell them so?
In this usurious, broken nation,
Where am I to go?
"I know in New York they tag bags
All black and labeled 'pet.'"
I told him, "I'm a pauper, tags
For rabies's all I get."

Told me, "There's no need to bag her,
Leave her in the road.
Sometimes they let us," he looked haggard,
"Burn the strays by load.
If we will label her a stray,
It will not cost a dime."
I said, "She came to us a stray.
It, in her way, will rhyme."

There isn't fight left in our dog.
Her ghost has left her sod:
A palindrome — a light in fog — a
Dog was, I saw God.

The Last Will and Testament of Mark Neuenschwander

In the heat of July I had said my goodbye.
Read his will. It said, "Carry my carcass
Through the swamp and the sand to the Dis-
en-ey Land
Sincerely, love Neuenschwander, Marcus."

Well it wasn't a thrill to receive such a will
When his family got gold and the horses.
Especially when one is a son of a gun
And another is buff special forces.

But without all his vinyls, his snuff box *tou
rhinal*,
I had no reward for amortise.
So I strapped on the body — my lifelong old
buddy —
And hitchhiked with Neuenschwander,
Marcus.

Now the truckers are suckers for bone-chilling
shuckers
They find out on route forty-four.
For some elders delight to renew such a sight
They ain't seen since the Vietnam War.

And the young men are shoddy to see such
a body
Then think: *podcasts*. True crime on their
minds.
But whatever the case, I shall bless human
race:
They all picked up both me and Mark's rinds.

Now the first thing the motorist asked me, the
votarist,
Why I would vow to drag Mark
Through the wind and the rain and my old
bunion pain
To the Disney of Walt's little park.

Well I said, "It's his testament; lifelong Mark's
estimate
Factored in considerations.
And this one he sacrificed till he met paradise:
Old-school midwestern vacations.

"He spent all moneys on arts and on funnies
And saved opting out of his knee

That the doctor named Cuminum saved for
aluminum
Swap, like they have down in Disney.

"So instead of life savings he went for his
cravings,
But still got in one final word.
And asked me, his buddy, to tie up his body
As if he's my backpack or sword.

"Now armed up with Marcus and girded with
carcass
I'm on this vacation for... *fun*?
He smells like a bunghole got filled with an
egg roll
That rotted in Ten-Ninety-One."

Well the truck driver dumped us and I
checked my compass
In case we met Marilyn Manson.
But I thought that we couldn't since the neon
said WOULDN'T
IT BE NICE TO GO TRAVEL TO
BRANSON?

I thought it was lame but Mark had some
acclaim
In the hillbilly version of Broadway.

So I shouldered the stiff and we hiked up the
cliff
And I prayed for the Reckoning Day.

Well it turns out the actors account for prayer
factors,
They'd put on a play by that name.
It was closing that night and The Raptured
set sight
On the carrion, knowing his name.

"Say old pilgrim," said one, "that's my favorite
son
From Old Joplin... what's left of his carcass.
Come on boys, help this puss on up into
our bus:
It's the body of Neuenschwander, Marcus!"

Well we travelled a ways with the old Branson
players,
I counted the trees and the quamash.
But then I and deceased knew we'd gone too
far east
Cause we landed surrounded by Amish.

Guess it turns out play pastors have twins in
Lancaster
And that plays — for the Amish — aren't "tech."

But the bearded old coachmen glanced down
at my roachman
And kicked me on out, "GO TO HECK!"

For the Gulf Shores the Arabs gave Gulf Wars
their spare ribs
So we might buy cute micey ears.
So I set my eyes south, put my hand in Mark's
mouth
Like a puppet: ventriloquized fears:

"Well old Lancey of Pantsy this dancey was
fancy
But soon all my skin will turn green.
And I wonder if maybe we get a bit lazy
And settle for Saint Augustine?"

My knuckles were pussy, so I became fussy
And said, "I have given my vow.
I have dragged your cadaver through pit stop
and tavern.
We two are not giving up now."

We boarded a sleeper on Amtrak. "*The
Reaper*"
They called me in Dining Room Car.
We made it to Jacksonville, land of the taxless
will,
Smelling of Devil's cigar.

From there a whole family of gators came
rapidly
Up to us both on the curb.
"Just give us the body and we won't be
naughty."
I said, "I am rather disturbed."

They look shocked that I mocked them, but I
kept on talking:
"I'd heard that you gators had couth.
You'd really revoke a poor dying man's joke
For the sake of a little sweet tooth?"

Well the gators weren't haters, but appre-
ciators,
They struck me a bargain instead:
They would never eat me and they'd let Mark
ride free
If we got them some Walt Disney bread.

Well we rode on the backs of the things who
thought snacks
Came in packages labeled "long pork."
Came at last a solution to our persecution,
Admittedly, this took some work:

They footed the bill for the sake of Mark's will

And me and Mark's body rode rides.
While the gators devoured for hours and
    hours
All the C.E.O.s, cosplays, and guides.

In the heat of July how I said my goodbye.
Read his will. It said, "Carry my carcass
Through the swamp and the sand to the Dis-
    en-ey Land
Sincerely, love Neuenschwander, Marcus."

Look at the Birds

Again Frank's sisters call to me
By chirping at the dawn
While all the dark is blushing pink
From stabbing Avalon.

On yesterday a devil dawn
Arose in several climes,
An omen for the wobegon
Whose pension oftentimes

Are daily logging loss by loss
From tyrant's tariff war.
He shot so many albatross,
He shot the metaphor.

And now the sisters call to me
As dawn will blush regret.
Look at the birds, their jubilee:

They hold no public debt.

They do not toil for meat and mead
Or gamble with our graves.
Ubiquitous as reel and bread,
Yet own and are not slaves.

But somehow feast while Yankees starve,
We foolish bourgeoise.
They feast and feed on not but parve:
Origination fee.

Grace

The gifts of the people
Of God for God
Were brought from the Zoro-
Astran men
Who studied the boretides
Of globes and gods
That starlit a journey
From east to East
Arrived when he's toddling
When three year olds
Are likely to tantrum
But this one made
A peacemaking pilgrim
Who climbed the hill
To carry the cross he'd
Learned how to carve
While Joseph was teaching
The woodsman's way.
And there on the skull
The babe of sages
Gave what he had taken:
The gifts of God
For the people of God.

Superhero Movings

As a generation rises
In the loam of supermen
All their phones have turned to cameras
All their deeds to corporate sins
As they get their bodies X-rayed,
Finger-printed, DNA'd,
And they feel the eye of Sauron
Substituted for a moron's
Archive every shit and bore on
Tablets made of younger men

Not always did the TSA
Exist for charter planes;
We once had only dogs outside
The metal-scaling party line
With every homebound flight on time
Without pat-down complaints

The homeland generation knows
Of Treyvon, Batman both,

Of Michael Brown and Spiderman
And incarnation jokes,
Of Guardians of Galaxies
And NYPD fallacies
Of quotas shipping coke.

The pain of hero's heroes
That our heroes never heed:
The pain of losing half their lives
For lighting up some weed.

Response to Being Complimented on my Reading Voice at the New York Poetry Festival

It isn't how they do it, see,
They droll and dogger on,
They speak as if exhuming words —
Analogy foregone.

Some MFAs and PhDs
have taught our poets, "Kill
Those living, breathing, metric things:
Chip symbols up in mills."

A poet ought not bore you, drug
You — voice-made-chloroform —
Good poems....

RUN YOU DOWN WITH BATS
AND BEAT YOUR FACE AND STOMP
  YOUR HATS
AND CAST THEIR PEARLS DOWN TO
  YOUR RATS

And teach sex-ed to BUREAUCRATS
And *abstinence* to nymphomaniacs
And make... *volcanos...* habitats
For igloos, thunderstorms,
And forms of
Prayer and *ladybugs.*

Two Rooms, One Mirror

I know a girl, my destination
worth a week of creation
who elated my life

Could you please help my situation
'cause I need an innovation
just to make her my wife

I've never met her but I've seen her through a
clouded mirror
I wish she knew it had two sides and get
over here
If I keep standing starin' stridin' steady 'round
the room
I think she'll notice me soon.

Life flows by stormy navigations
but my overcompensations

...I
...I
hesitated twice

She came to a sudden realization
She listened, heard my station
So I shook up the dice

By slowly turning she had thought she saw my
figure there
If I would break the mirror she'd startle but
I'd have a prayer
But I kept holding honor, holdin' hope, and
holdin' on
To think she'd shatter our dawn...
and I wouldn't have to...

Rain dropped from the ceilings preparation
To annihilate salvation
Could I save her from a crime?

I threw a brick in combination
With an axe in desperation
Just to save her in time

Her room kept flooding as she saw me try to
save her life

I fin'lly broke the mirror to hold my lifeless
almost-wife
I'll never love her, never kiss her, never hold
her hand
She'll never marry this man

Braille

When night sex—lips to lips—
When wind hits open hands—
When whitecaps wash right over feet
that stand on laundered sands.

When chocolate after fasts—
When noodles for the poor—
When children who have found their meal
will beg *summore, summore.*

Mere inches from the lawn
my nose on what's been mowed—
Or bottled wines — or siloed grains
when smell of what's been sowed.

When symphonies unsung
before the present time—
When sudden lyrics overheard
disclose a metric rhyme.

Away

I spent my childhood
    in the creekbed

that met great river
    that met a greater river

I was a swimmer,
    but I dreamt of a raft:

I know how to sail Crooked Creek
    to Kasskasskia to Mississippi

to Atlantian waters
    in search of hissing secrets.

Reticence

Later silence
is what
makes sex
an inside joke.

Smoke Alarm

Burp, burp
　　with chirp
　　my sister thinks

as making
　　noises like
　　a hungry bird

too is my niece.
　　Unthinking
　　the words

I'd planned
　　if, like batteries,
　　she'd died.

Fragile

Day after day,
    one black bootstrap hangs

from the wire
    of our phone line.

I find it surprising
    that no phone line tech

has ever planted
    tulips in those boots

Partisan

It's also
embracing foes

that *is*
holding

your loved
ones close.

Brooklyn Song

Hot smoke on the other
    pane of the argon.

A cold sheet on
    this pane of my night.

No matter how
    tired the city is,

it's still Sleepless.
    Like last night

when my CPAP
    mask tore

and I nearly choked
  to death because

corps hoard instead
  of living their job.

I would have been better
  choking on wildfire smoke.

That's why I write
  poems in Greenwood

by leaving
  my house.

Collateral

I feel his ankle
then I feel
his other ankle

it's due to playing
superempath daily
with the original

feels. These are
why the whole
world hurts:

Everyone walks
around with a hole
blown in their chest

when someone they
know who was
sprained to death.

Native Summa

I would have liked
  to have seen Cahokia

in its prime
  mounds of empire

while Thomas Aquinas
  wrote his summa.

Objection:
  "It seems there was no empire."

I answer that:
  Some things are not *because* they were killed.

Elegy for a Carpenter

The Bells of St. Theresa twenty-once
Will ring now ever slower till he sighs
his final feeble wind, both bane and bunce,
Far better than our guns the belfry cries:

"The hammer was a stone before the knife,
The hammerfell was heard in Camelot
By Smith and Knight and Drummer near the
Fife,
Before e'en wedge, the hammer's first in
thought.

"Before we wielded wheel or gun or blade,
Before the books and coats we made of roan,
Before our hearth, glue, loom, bread, kiln man-
made
The hammerfell we struck on wood and bone."

Now twenty-once the hammer strikes the bell
And from it ring the roofs in Illinois,
The sound of hammerfell in town and dell,
Of hammers striking gables, Jerry's noise.

He walked our roads of mud and dirt
and sand
Until we paved them, shale and chip and
stone.
He walked and talked to God as fairyland
Makes men see soul in sod, turn stumps to
thrones.

He'd stop for stout and story, prayer and joke,
He'd stop for gossip, sympathy, and news,
He'd stop to hear you, hurt or hardy folk,
He'd listen, love, then carry on bemused.

They loved him for his humor and his homes.
They loved him for his honesty and smile.
He'd work on loves till never unfulfilled
The bonds he'd tied with men and women,
threads

Of cords the Lord had woven in the stores
Of hardware all around South Illinois
Like belts inside a handmade chest of drawers
Are loves he tied to things he built, his joy:

On deathbed Jerry's hands swung hard on
hinge.
They asked him, "Whatcha doing, Daddy
love?"
He said, "I'm building." Hammered, tied, and
cinched.
"Where at?" they asked.
"In heaven up above."

So when the St. Theresa bells ring out
Another toll and slower till you die
And rise to winds up there from hereabout
And get a body, new, up in the sky:

You'll see those gates of pearl and streets of
gold,
You'll see the shops of diamond, flame, and
jade,
You'll smell the cedar, redwood, hewn of old
For kingly halls the Schaubert Co. has made.

It's not a smith or soldier or a spy
Who prepped a place for us before return,
But Christ the carpenter of soul and sky
Whose ownership we tenants now attorn:

But how did Christ once master hammerfells?

And where did Christ discover wood and
nail?
And who taught Christ to whittle masterful?
To know which hawthorne shelters, which
impales?

Defers it to the maker, Father God.
Defers it to sustainer, Holy Ghost.
He learned it from the virgin womb
unmarred.
He learned it most from manful corner posts:

For Joseph could have left God's mom alone,
For Joseph could have taught God other
trades,
For Joseph could have left our Christ at home,
Instead he showed how hammerheads beat
blades:

What is it like to teach adopted son
Along with holy family handicraft?
To watch your child cross boards now one-by-
one,
To turn cross-sections of a house to haft

Of weapon, tool, or something older still:
The handle of the universe in hand?
For if he holds the whole world in his will
He wields it by a hilt he melted, manned,

And beat into a cross-guard by the head
Of hammerfells he learned from carpentry.
From building home for living, tombs for
dead,
He learned to build our heaven's blooming
tree.

Did Joseph know how he'd adopted death?
Did Joseph see the torture in the thorns
Of hawthorns sanded or the splinter's wreath?
Did Joseph know the loincloth's robe, though
worn?

Did Joseph know two tiny wrists that nailed
Two boards together would become said
boards?
Did echoes of the christchild's younger wails
Grow in his ear: the death cry of his Lord?

When Jesus crossed his boards, nailed one-by-
one,
Did Joseph flinch and think of Roman
swords?
When Jerry nailed two two-by-fours as one,
Did Jerry feel the dying of his Lord?

Did Jerry feel the fluid in Christ's lung?

The skin so parched it too was pained by
thirst?
Did Jerry too gape mouth and twitch his
tongue
For sponge on stick and whispering, "I thirst"
?

And when the carpenter of heaven's gates
Rewards old Jerry with a body new
His arm will once again drive nails in slates
And sand and saw and plane, wrench, level,
screw.

Saw Joseph this in wood and nail and saw
When Christ built prophecy from kiddie
tools:
Cross-sections, cross-guards, hammerhead
and claw,
the Infant God nailed wisdom into fools.

"Prepare a place." He promised roof and stud.
The Foreman of the Firmament prepares.
Now Jerry's on God's crew by water, blood,
And sawdust. Glad he got a kick upstairs.

Processional

The bear priest came
Carrying the rough hard wood
Of the wild processional cross
And the alpine parted ways
To make straight the path
Leveling Adirondacks
Raising Silver Bay.

You think I'm frigging nuts.
Fine.
You think it's a t-shaped
Power line.
But I know how long those
Things last when well-kept
By utility monopolies and
Filled with electrons moved by petrol.
They crack, fall, splinter in hinter ice
Shatter in tornados.
Then what?

This one?
It has no lines, no power.
Only the hard wood of the processional crosses
And still the branches have eclipsed in
The pine needles, have parted
Waxed gibbous the apophatic
And all the trees of the field
—have covered their blush
—will clap their hands
—didn't interrupt

Yes, horns still walk the Greenwood lands
In the north of New York
And kneel for
The hardwood
Of the man who can
Hit a straight lick with a crooked stick

Treebeard

The light through the towers
Of ancient deciduous
Hits the gratuitous
Red of the maple,
Young, different at different
Times of the day.

It is not unlike red beard
Of the photographer
From Whiskerino
(The beard growing competition)
Who took a self
Portrait each day
At different times; ways
From the same angle

So grows and goes the red
Maple leaves
In the lace of moving sun
In the grid of mid-morning

In the interdigitation of noon
An the resulting house lights
In the watercolor wash fading to bright gold
In the spotlight of tea time
And in the will-o-whisps of every
One tree in a day does not move
Yet still shows her pilgrimage

Had I known this
I would have taken a self-portrait
Of my face's bark
Day after day after day
Till death do us party.

Often; Briefly — do people find it

A bridge of stars
Connects the city on a hill
With the dark track of our
Rumbling

Evenly spaced suns,
Each a navigator in its own light,
So that they shine and
Is that snow?
A ski slope beneath the skyway?
No.

It's the Hudson.
What a relief:
I really am on the straight and narrow home,
aren't I?

Waking

How glorious! I preach of the mind
And eight birds take flight from their trees and
Flee the city. Eight more land near me
To hear and heed. I preach on the bone, the ghost,
The grey parrot, the willow weep, leaves
Of silver maples ass-up for storm alerts,
Harmonics, the music of the spheres, heavenly choirs
Heard at dawn — seven swans fly away
And crest the Catskill mountain.s
Eight eagles land, but they're clucking
Angry chickens. Eight more go still,
I am just a noisy bear, a loud bobcat.
Logos is present, for these as meter in
Maples, harmonics in holly. They know growth,
The increase, the heavy — the black cave brighten
The deeps made delvable — the second
The Logos open his eyes against the Sandman
Takes stock, takes wind. And tells
The old, old story again and again and again...

Charism

This morn, a coin
In this navy
Slung
An uncountable set

Of slowly lathed beams into
This vale, in which
Two thousand feet away, I happened
to be sipping, sitting.

I didn't know
What gold had come —
The bomb or magic or the great bowed
Apollo of old —

He was that hidden. Yet, anyhow,
There come seconds
Where the metaphor is hiding merely

From sight. Snow fell yesterday

So much donut glaze
Over the mountain's trees
And on this April camp
You'd have thought it was there

For us to see how Bob Ross
Would have painted it, then melted.
Another poet would reify it,
Charged the beaches, crossed Lake George,

Hiked the peaks
To find the coin — the gold, I mean.
But I am here before the surprise
Gilding of the lounge, staring at the warm

Charismatic hands out to the ghosts
Of the snow and whatever will shine.
I see the sacred mystery that
Unlike all the others, is no revealed secret.

Were Mary Oliver Here

Boy throws stone in Mountain River Creek
—
Were Mary Oliver here
She would talk about how one life
Ripples the morning calm
Revealing every other shore —
But that assumes the universe is calm.

For Mary isn't here anymore
Her ripples were swallowed by cosmic
currents.
When springs from hidden Catskill Heights
Tumble down ten thousand borrowed stones
The stones the boy throws splashes
Yes
But the splash is swallowed
Cataract
For eye and water both
No trace of impact, influence, life
Gone in the ever falling tempest

I despair for my dad
How quick he'll be forgotten
When the cataract of time
Blinds it to my own mind and memories

The boy does not.
He simply — pooh-like — picks a stick
And throws it in the waves

It too is swallowed for a time
But water — after plunge and under bridge
It surfaces from the sunken stones
And floats — the ill seeker — down
the mountain to Lake George's Silver Bay
Where — dammit, Mary, you were *right* —
It runs aground on golden shores.
And I, weeping, am stuck with silver
While Mary waits for me.

APPLICATION FOR THE WRITING EXCUSES SCHOLARSHIP

My first app came in letter,
My second as a tale,
But neither fruited scholarship
For writing whilst set sail.

So now I write a ballad
To appeal to all the clan
Who speak of M.I.C.E. and worsening
Protagonists's adversities
And beefing up diversities
In tales of mice and man.

I'd love to learn from fellow writers,
Speakers, nerds, and more.
I'd die to meet the makers
Of the worlds that I explore.

But most of all I'd love to give

To those who gave to me:
To fold their tables, sort their signs,
To sweep, to lift, to see

Their every need and meet them
On their cruise of verse and prose,
To heed and help and lend some hope
From poverty and woes:

I have no great connections,
No state-school-stamped degrees.
I live below the poverty line
with Brooklyn's crooked trees.

In eight long generations
My diploma from my school
Is the highest education
My family of fools
Could dream of as improvement
— bachelor's as bereavement
For the poor and underschooled.

I've no more commendations,
I hold no pence or pound.
No reference letters have I saved,
I only own the words I gave:
Their temper, tale, and sound.

But still I'd love to come and learn,
And still I'd love to heed
The sorts of things that shade your ink
And fill you up so that you drink
Of deeper wells than doublethink.
For whom your hearts still bleed?
For these I too would *burn*.

But voiceless will I never stay.
First sample well, then enter fray:
I drink deep, think, before I write —
Ice turned flame (meteorite):*
**To "meteor" rhyme, first quench said light*

For writers, there, of fictions
I'd help with my convictions:
I know how Brandon fought for magic
With elder pros (who thought him tragic:
Wrongness, bold). Pelagic
Retreat now assumes his dictions
and his laws of magic fictions.
Tales of writers with convictions
Are Advant-Garde-turned-classic.

I need some fellow pilgrims
For the writing life is long.
It's good and gracious when you're poor
And probably great, I guess, when yóu're
Well paid for every song.
Oh Bestseller Civillians,
I want my ink and page, not billions,

And friends who sing along.

That's all, I guess, I'm asking you
Who run this thing, who turn a cruise
To Canterbury on the sea:
That writer folk like you, like me,
Have need of peer review.

Three years I've applied.
(Two brushed aside.)
I ask you: please. Now Mockingbirded
Starry Nighted, Christ begirded,
I'll keep trying, undeterred, and
Each app intensify.
Tight apps like this you've seldom heard: end-
To-title, four-fifty words.

What they Neglect to Mention about the Vatican

The red paint of frescos fade
With the drips of water drops
As caverns shift positions
The paintings' dance don't stop.

The steel braces bleed their rust
And the copper sickly greens
While all the towers whisper
Of their dying, buried things.

The high thoughts men are thinking —
Have thought two-thousand years —
They rest in paint about the drawers
And sculpted devils, kings, and boars
Like the mind of God in the hearts of whores
Preserved in gold veneers.

For reason predicates this Rome

— Her math and talk and song,
Her logic and astronomy
And rhetoric, agronomy,
Philosophy, theology,
And laws of right and wrong —

The mind of God in heads of men
Made permanent this paint,
Preserved the marble from the storm,
The priesthood from both sin and worm,
And still makes sinners saints.

For Rome was resurrected
From the bomb and spear and loss,
For God returned to earth in pain
By highest thoughts some think insane —
All Genius took an infant brain —
And he whispered of a coming rain:
First flood his home, then bloom again,
When the Maker took the cross.

Joplin Sunsets

I stand above New Jersey
In a bungalow in clouds.
We face the old Manhattos —
Their dawn and misty shrouds.

Iclandic-bound photographer
Has left our little home.
I wish he had a Cessna here
To capture cranes and foam.

I wish it were a sunset
In Ozark looking west.
The New York smog is not the dust
at Kansas's behest.

The colors of my memory
When nineteen years I'd lived
Are ringing in my travelogue,

Are ringing — coins she gived

To coffers of experience
Analogy of kids:
Success is like new furniture
And death their auction bids.

Tectonic Shift

When growing up in Salem
My friends had many skills
And perks and treasures, trips to beaches,
mountains, woods, and hills.

I didn't have a dollar
I didn't have a dime
I didn't have a title, pennant,
championship or rhyme

I didn't keep a steady job
Inherit some estate
Attract a girl or even boys
Or make my city great

I didn't sell a painting
I didn't drink much beer
I didn't try for politics

for power was my fear

I had no honor nor no fame
I wrote no holy writ
For many friends would bully me:
few teachers gave a shit

But now I'm old and now I see
what wealth and honor lay
inside the blinds of family
in every friendship's way.

I miss the murk of dark abyss
That lay beneath the lakes.
I miss the fields cause towers, trains,
And bridges feel the quakes.

When burned, you give us balm

When burned, you give us balm,
When drowning, breath of God,
When falling through the air you catch us,
Rock in sinking sod.

Betrayed, we feel your trust,
Suspected —just like you—
Worn thin, you make us hearty,
fill us up until we're true.

Oh hidden lightning spark
that quickens every corpse
ignite our minds with motives true
and beauty like the Lord's.

When lonely, you're our guard.
When broken — mortar, glue —
When cut, you're gauze, when tired, a pillow,

Jazz when we are blue.

Remind us every down
descends until your peak:
Though demons climb infernal mountains
Splash up high their fiery fountains,
upside's down, for low amounts
to heights for heaven's meek.

Pangolin Lover

I once alone was riding Hawthorne Road
when something told me stop, to leave
  my load
a cottage stood across that crooked way
the other side: a mansion (marble maze)
I knocked upon the cottage, there to wait
until a pangolin swung wide the gate.

I followed her to garden's weedy soil
and offered her my presence, mind, and toil —
the pangolin, she took no aid from me.
She pointed to the empty house, the tree:
her friends at camp, her family work and play,
and she alone: I could not help that day.
"I wish you well," I said and then, "please call
if ever you need a friend or neighbor,
I'm happy to show, though I'm a stranger."

I hear she's living in Africa, stays
and tends a garden where pangolins play.

She seeks the good, the beautiful, the true
wherever found beyond sky, ocean blue,
and true things, good, and beautiful all fall
into a unity. Friends, they have shown,
and family and more: how now she calls

another "pangolin lover"
in the garden, on the clover,
with the open above and firm below,
(not a hawthorne maze or a crooked road).
On that spot heard her "Stop and leave your load,"
For pangolins laying along her way
needed her help and her home and her play.

(It isn't so bad to travel alone
if you know how to stop and leave your load.)

Let it be

Of all people
Madeline L'Engle

wrote upon her desk
while bowing her head:

"The deepest message
of the incarnation

is there is nothing
so secular

that it cannot
be sacred."

Seeking Truth,
seeking Beauty,

seeking Goodness
is prayer

since these too
are names of God.

Riddles

what has a ring that must be fingered,
has a head where thought won't linger,
has a neck can't breathe, can break,
has a bridge: no road, creek, lake?

what walks on scales yet weighs but little,
starts out squishy, ends up brittle,
name's erotic (in the mood),
and is a special kind of food?

What has a cap but ain't a head,
can rise but once when it is dead,
unlike good food is bad when filling,
wielding dogged or inciting milling?

What empties, fills and leaks a bit
and calls its neighbor full of shit?

What has lace but isn't fabric,
loved by banker and by maverick,
filled with eyes but ain't a bug,
long of tongue but cannot hug?

What is needed first, then counted,
can't be hammered, synced, or mounted,
should not share a single basket,
often guts become its casket?

What has paper, not a press,
buttons, zippers, not on dress,
has a throne but not a king,
goldless though with bar and ring?

What hears begging in the summer,
in the fall sounds like a drummer,
in the winter's still as grave,
springtime sings to king and slave?

What can't spin but is a top,
must be cleaned by rag and mop?

What's no lineman yet still blocks,
has no market but has stocks,

strips down naked 'fore it leaves,
turns to strainers, is not sieves?

What has a coat but isn't cold,
cannot feel the touch of mold,
wrinkled skin but not a beast,
loved by greatest and the least?

Sonnet of a Siren's Sorrows

The other ladies envy how I look:
my sea-through linens, white made light by
mist,
my sun-bleached hazel hair, my body's book
Read right by now-dead sailors. How I've
missed
The men who came to me, who heeded songs
I sang form-fit, an ear apiece: a dirge
For Dirk, a hymn for Henry — right or wrong
—
That steered their ships to smash upon my
ridge.

Girls: envy not my slaying (*lust by hope*),
My Sehnsucht seems too much for men of
skin.
For I desire Desire behind desires
While they desire not longing, but to grope
At straws of puberty as if to win
The Love of loves by burning Fire with fires.

The Joplin Options

Well if you climb up mountains
Store your gravel in a vat,
Then you'll need to come to Joplin
Where we trod on gorgeous chat.
For our chat is like the desert
But without that snowing sand
And it's tall like Mt. McKinley
(But less racist and less grand).
It's the leavings from the minings
Where we left our fathers dead,
But less toxic than their corpses
Cause it's only filled with lead.

Oh and if you like Niagara
You will love our Great Big Falls
For Niagara's fresh and flowy
And ours holds some Castrols.
Well I wouldn't like to stand in it
Unless my feet need glass
And I wouldn't like to sit on it
With where I pass my gas.
But it's beautiful to look at

And it smells of sea and fish,
Water rising every evening
From that copper, nickel wish
That, well, you and all your buddies
Tossed as if in Trevi Fount
But your wishes all die with you.
(Plus you've flushed your bank account.)

We have so many restaurants
That our restaurants pick the bones
Of the restaurants that ate restaurants
Like a restaurant Game of Thrones
Like the time the Bearded Lady
And some other local Jones
Picked the leavings of the building
That we used to call Caldone's

Unless you count the highway
Or monopolies of spark,
Unless you count the hillside
Kept by monks we call Ozárk,
Unless you count tornados, parks,
Our building-steeple chase,

We're less about our landmarks.
We're more a people place.

Threnody for Granny

4 A.M. I rise unresting
As the deer at dawn.
Mind on images arresting:
Mother, Amazon.
From its storehouse sobbing loosed:
Dread alone had bound
It to the tree of Death, a fruit.
Wished it: *never ground.*

She: bacon's morning herald,
Frying turned to war.
She: granddaughters her emeralds
Bankrupt giving shore
From Indiana lakeside —
Spite and Malice rounds,
Marlboros, and Fascination,
Pitch black coffee grounds.

You think the grave will hold her?
She the bane of bats?

She whose voice is morning thunder?
Tower shields for hats?
What great causes she gave grandsons
Sleep for now in Christ —
Hospitality and ransoms,
Ham and melon, sliced.

She is nearer than our words
Wasted on her now.
Near in thunder, coffee, birds,
Darke Fair's cane and sow.
Had we but a little faith
We would see the cloud
Of witnesses now real, not wraiths,
Shining hind the shroud:

Next to Patrick, Frank, and Paul
There sits a little girl
Who never lost her voice at all,
Whose hair has kept its curl.
She who bore our world in womb
Now younger, holds a hand
That holds the gold and cross and tomb
And every grain of sand.

Presents soon will rise high tide
Piling round the pine
That roots the world's Christmastide.
Her pictures wrapped and twined.
The Word unknown, unspoken
Knows now, speaks to us:

His great crossword unbroken.
BIC gripped by charlotte russe—

Her lady fingers filling
Blanks between the blacks.
Newer songs unknown by Dylan.
(Her view parallax—
She sees our objects closer
Than even we can see).
She hears the great composer's
Songs of victory.

Now she knows the Hence and Hither
From Whom all has gone;
Sparrows fall, lilies wither,
Yonder known by Yon;
All the Want behind her wants,
Longing known above;
Knows if love be want to wonder
wandering to Love.

Some men think she waits ahead
Cheering at The End,
Some men think the sleeping dead
Will bolt from Heaven's pen.
But good men know human soul's
Naught without some bone.
Her body, mind, will sprout with others
From what Word was sown.

That Word, for her, on white stone
Her true name is her key
The Locksmith holds, unlocks her heart —
Each person's mystery.
For there was never one like her
Nor never will there be
Mother, Daughter, Sister, Soldier.
Sally forth, Granny.

See she has one more granddaughter
Courtney up above
Yet to taste her dunkey eggs,
Feel her ursine hug,
Yet to ride Durango runners,
Smell her Shalimar.
Courtney must catch up with Granny,
Then they'll pack the car:

For there is one Eternal Summer
Yet within our reach
Where Granny, Courtney, others wait
On Indiana Beach.
There the ski boats need no gas,
Kiddos cut the fries,
Corn hole tourneys last and last,
They never close the rides.

New Neighbors

This green haven I know
Bears evidence of new neighbors:
Maybe I should bring some flowers?
Welcome them to their new digs?

Twenty-five muddy patches
I saw on my ascent to Samuel Morses's pillar
No more graves left to rent

Will And Testament burials
Deeded to die here by family left
Worded to die not by Corona

It's louder in Greenwood
Sobs echo in barrowdowns
Children skip, enmasked, among the pink, the
    white
Tulip trees

Climbing bay and beech
Soldiers of sprouts. Spies of saplings. Tinkers
    of twigs
Tailors mending a tomorrow
Sewing seeds in a patchwork quilt.

To: Lance

Someone left the window open
Left the stained glass wide
So inside the silent cloister
Brooklyn noise abides
It is darkness in the courtyard
Hamilton is loud
All I see inside the mirror
There reflected in the smearer
Through my trembling screen and fear:
A marble son in shroud.

One star someone shines on Mary
And their light has now
Made it past the screen and colors
Cage and branch somehow:

Only on this night this angle
Only in this heat
Only if in silence I was
Stopped by noisy street

Only with a mirror here
The women's room for me
Only with the sable seams
Of stained glass now and then
Only with the Gardner's pruning
Only in this light
Did what's Needful carve a symbol
Just for me tonight?

CANOPY PRAYERS

The windows of the monastery
Greenwood's filling up
A flower tree of branch and green
Like hard green tea in cup.

It barren rose in winter months,
But now has soused my view.
And what would be annoying hunts
Is visually new:

It is as if the monastery
Now is treehouse bright.
The rainforest prayer of canopy
Is shadow, verdant light.

I want my pray a treehouse
With every waking step.
I want to have a living vista

Giving strolls a pep.

For if the drudgery of sidewalks
Has a canopy
The joy of tongue and mind will talk
As far as you can see

To fill the hearing of the urban
Faces in a dream
To turn the black of city life
To stained glass sable seams.

A Reversion to the Mean

A Storm Assaults the Stained Glass of Greenwood Chapel

The glass goes dark and the green field
Behind the unhidden hope of the risen
Fades from frame. The frames are black.
The seams slacken and the sudden glories
— of the time my cousin took her life
And the time my wife woke temper —
When the words and signs in the windows
    carried
Me back to broken, born again
And again and again in the gate of poems
And prophetic furies. Funny how a snow
Or a hard heavy heavenly raining
Will erase the rumors you really wanted
And replace their prose with the perfect word:

Stained glass seams. Sable cracks,
Yet to seal the scenes. A surge and another
hits the hues, how it soaks,
Till the words in the window weep their
    symbols:
Rivers from "life," "resurrection" a wet thing.

Even the early eaves of white
Chapel stonework can change their reflection
To the dark grey of dirge played
Light and lithe, and loam and stone
Is readied for the rising of ruined buried
Things that grow grey there in the dark.
Light under heavy. Listen to the rain
Stuck in the glass. Streams in the weeds.
Blood in the bones and breath in the dust.

Was it always this white?

The old birch trees go always grey.
These are those from thou youth
And my childhood. But Greenwood chased
Me to the north — to a new Lake:
George and the Y of the geriatrics.
Silver Bay has Born Limbs
And broken birch branches down
So that my bride picked a pretty thing
For a walking stick — straight bleach bark.
It tumbles into ten perfectly trimmed logs
As if Wolverine had whacked it thrice.

Some years we are young about
In memory. Some make us
Young for the first and final time:
Albino ents where the old grey'd gone.

Few Unshorn

The rain renders the Adirondacks
Grey and grizzled. Seldom have I glanced
At a ridge to see how a single tree
Stamps its name in the Nirvanac bliss
Of upper skies. Early the chin
Of the sleeping mountain titan slickened
But for where he forgot to wield the razor
And left alpine stubble alone
For me to find. It's a kind of magic
To see your late father sleeping
Across Silver Bay and its sea.
Alive only long enough
For Greenwood to grip my grin and mouth
And shake loose my, "Look Papa:
You missed a spot. Good morning."
Before my dad is dead again,

Still Schaubert cheeks stick to Schaubert teeth
Where his grip had grabbed my growing
    stubble.

Thunderbird

The thunderstorm streams in a rain bomb
Into the reeds and clear islets,
Washing from waters to waters again.
You will think that it fell thunderous
From a cumulonimbus. But the nimbus
  of sun
Has limned each tree with liquid golden
Hour again. So great was the rain,
Where else could it emerge? Maybe you'll
  focus
On the wings of the heron who took weather
With him into air. I would have missed
The storm wall in the wings of that fowl
Had he neglected to turn, glistening bank,
Gracing the waters with waters again.

I refuse to believe that future rainstorms
Happen any other way.

THE HORROR OF PROVIDENCE

The ghost goes in the grey smoke,
High above and built of steel.
A Thunderbird ghost in the thick of the night
Carries its light, carries its torch,
Carries its flashlight over the porches
Of Brooklyn stoops, a ray in the fog.

I hammer my umbrella into the heights
Of every boxed-in elm and cherry,
But not the dogwood, he's suffered enough.
I rap it to knock the rain loose
That didn't wait for me to walk.

The R isn't running around Brooklyn.
I could take the D, but something told me
"Stride up the hill to the B63."
There I pray and bid the barkeep good e'en.
After a time, I test the route:
It's there in ten, then thirty-five

To drive me home. "Forty-five
To walk home is healthy enough."

I let my mind wander as I might've
In my younger days. I take in the yew,
I rattle my umbrella, I greet a roar —
Another ghost, a nightbird goes
Carrying the fire in a clean beam.

Almost an hour for the bus to even
Catch me by Sunset Park in the cool.
I have greeted Greenwood, whose gates are
    asleep,
And noticed now there is not one fence
But two: a black iron and a stone.
Leave them alone one alerts me,
Leave them the other repeats to the alone.

But why am I walking? Why this urge?

Up Sunset I climb with the city behind,
Past evening athletes earning their scores
In football and volleys. My feet carry me
To the corner exit beneath ghosts in climax
To see an old man bowed in hunch.

Drunk enough to drop on his face
Bleeding profusely. Bleerily eyed.
Insisting no ambulance, swaying like those
 dogwoods
During the rainstorm that missed me in my
 writing.
(The storm wall in the wings of that fowl
Gracing the waters with waters again.)

I walked him across the crosswalk in time.
Left him alone cause he wanted left.

Two blocks later, I tell you *I heard*:

"Were this your Grandpa Remmy, then
 think."

"I'd turn around," I told the voice.

It took two blocks backtracking,
Another half to catch this elder.
Three more blocks to bring him home.

But walking him three blocks away

Cost me nothing. Nary a poem.
Merely a "Speak, Lord, your servant will
listen."

This, to me, is what we mean
When we preach on providence.

Automobile Fences

The mist remade all the motley lights
of the night cruisers in their ninety cars
to so many shattered disco stars.
Pile ups don't happen overnight,
but they did then. The dark fog
rendering every little rider —
from fender bender to fractured soul
to mangled mother and mutilated trucker —
to a true disaster: ain't no stars
fixed anymore. So he foolishly left
his car to seek shelter. Might have been
    clipped.

He jogged through the magic of apparated
    junkyard
dodging the still oncoming "drivers"
until he came to the guardrail's cold
folded steel, freaking its curves
with bloody knees. Normally folks
find themselves crushed between fencerow
and hood ornament, harrowed by grill.

He saw the fog and started to climb
but providence — or proffer the term —
yours — for the transcendent — yearned him
    other:
he waited, still. The fog withered
and on the other side of the guard opened
the maw of the abyss. He pocked his mouth,
koi out of the graveyard's old koi pond.

A man once said, "If you stumble on a fence
and want to move it, walk away
and think for a while. If you can wonder
    and tell
me why it was made, what it was for,
I will consent to you sundering its trusses,
barbed wire and welded studs."

We Americans love moving guardrails
in the fog and pileups of our freezing night.

Gumline

The river's soft gumline recedes.

What I mean is I'm used to muck banks,
To mud ramps and squished marshes,
Swamp trees with shallow trenches,
Sand dunes and high drops
Where we swung from rope to river's deep.

The river's soft gumline recedes —
All of that was eaten away, I think.
For all I see is the mountain of soil
Holding the birches and hugging the pines
Until two feet above the tame
Water line is weathered stone:
Not rocks or sand or mud or soil,
But a white line of grizzled bone
Like our game glitched and the great cave
Layer of Minecraft lurched in the wake.
It would be nice for my toes and neat.

(I should brush a bit sweeter
For a drought will come dark again.)

CROW CROSSES

Crow crosses the crater of death
Where the black and blue river
Styx separates the winter stems
And winterizing oaks and cedars,
A channel of oil, a blackberry stream,
And disappears in the dithering cattails.

Were it not so yellow I'd yell in the Amtrak —
Had it been blackened fire or the blight
Or the tall grass of the tiger climes,
I'd have shouted at the shrieking thing.

As it was, I ember and ash smoldered,
Wondering what portent so pitilessly soon
After I stopped with my father's estate.
What now? And what now?
And what what what could it be now?

Winberi

The contingency of things tames the most
prideful:
How source of sources seals the mind
And the origin of all origins is the sweet
Behind my smoothie. For the Huckleberry's
life
Came from its elders: coming pistulas
To stamen the seeds. See the fruit
Blooming from bees by Bach as he writes?
Or Vivaldi's rite vernal beside
The Huckleberry bush? How can a plant
Dead for ages deed being
To my smoothie's sweet? See: the gift
Of existence zips ziggurats like hot
Pants and folds the pleats so the feats
Of slaves and pharaohs slackens to nothing
And we realize at every red moment
The green and golden gifts and details
Of the little lives we lead can fade
Into nothing as such. Nearer my God
To Thee cries the thick açai
Berry and ice in the brazen sun
Before it sinks, before I sips
the binding rings, Precious.

The contingency of things tames the most me.

Cormorant upon the Styx

Schools of minnows scrape in a whip
like blue cookie dough in a Kitchen
Aid done up in Darke County.
Comes surfacing, the cormorant, black,
waits to hunt and dives in a wash.

And we wait and watch patient.

Too patient for air or a birdheart pulse.

A linger longer is what Lucas Roughly's
childhood church named chairs and tea
after service. See the cormorant?
Not yet have ye? It's a Ye Eld
Linger Longer. Lapse in the breath,
death in the bone. Where is the bird
who was diving? Where is the feather
that flew on the waves? How long can

waiting go, water crow?

You will think there's a turn, a truth like a
sonnet.

The prestige of the trick is we tried forever
to watch it surface. Sec: no bird.
No haunt of a bird. Neither here nor there
nor...

I can only conclude the cormorant shadow
disappeared
or
drew its shade
into its surest form: the wereshark.

My Sister's Dog's Birthday Party

My grandfather greets the grey scrubbed
Nurses and the night. Nicotine and smoke
He ought to have inhaled, once you consider
How asbestos beats your bronchia and air
    sacks
With C.O.P.D. "I could sleep on a nail"
He says to my bride. She smiles and writes
It all down for me. Ever wonder
Why we spend our summers in the sure
    blissful
Distance of friends who do not keep
The kind of spirit kindred that dads
And grandfathers gathered and the great
    pranks
Of all my brothers, all my sisters,
All of my cousins, and all of my mothers
Surrogate or Caesarian? You show up to your
Sister's puppy's smash birthday
Party and the people who please you there
And they look long and they love and smile
And you — for one — yearn to feel it,
To know you are loved so near home
That it hurts to realize your house thousands
Of miles away makes enough space

For a handful of friends: home is where
Hearts are seldom for home is the rest
Of the heart whose hope is rewarded
With homecoming and happy, healthy tears
Of the joy of pajamas and jars of canned
Green beans that the grace of last
Autumn offered and opened spring
Brunch at grandma's, bounty and brethren.

The Hunter and the Harrowing

The Hunter told us of the Harrowing he met
Over his last five buck lager
in the Bellhammer Bar and Grill's backyard:

"They never at night needed to enter
The unlit awning of their ancient house
After a drawn-out, dreadful quest.
They rather would strike its pillars with sticks
And rattle the shutters and shatter a rock
To scare the thing that scarce would leave
Without the stonesounds stonebears hate.
Without shouts or shuttered gates.
Without the light of an Easter lamp
Or the waters of Bashan showered on the
    jamb.
Enough moment and element
Then the harrowing would flee. So they
    hoped.
That's why they preferred the thankless out-
To the in-door midnight. Ever maddening,
They left open the screen and awning

Until every candle in the cottage was on.
So they asked me to come with my axe.
I did not strike its pillars with sticks
Or rattle its shutters or shatter its rocks,
For I wanted to sneak on the snarky harrow
Without the light of an Easter lamp
In anything but my thinker's heart.
In silence came the Harrowing crimn,
Shrieking only when it understood
I was there on purpose: It.
And still its shrieks shattered my ears.

I'd sharpened my axe with the wheel of Om.
I'd cut the thing not with my cleaving,
But rather with my heart for leaving it rent.
When I swung I expected to swish the air
And dodge before the axehead felled
The finest feet for fleeing there.

Yet air I did not find in the air.
I found instead the feeling of striking
Matted hair and mottled blood
And fermentation's fleabit brood
As leather, bone, and larder split
To loose the smell of layered smog.

And there I fainted till I freely woke.
I've often wondered Whether I
Cut it with mind or cut it with metal.
I'll never know."

Neither would we
As we sipped our last saisons
And slipped out, one at a time,
Silently walking to our little shacks,
Leaving our lonely cars in the lot.

Suptropic Architects

Would-have-been studs structure the grid
Where the grapes will grow or the olive groves.
Everything open to light and old winds
Flushing the bloodsuckers, flensing the
    rattlers.

If there is a vice, it's the vice of the nudist.
If there is a virtue, it's virtuous nudes.
The vulnerable shelter an elemental shade:
Exposed to the needful, awning from pain.

The people I've seen who stay open
The way these buildings wage freeness
Room and board in Liberty's bay:
If they have a vice, it's the vice of the nudist;
If they have a virtue, it's virtuous nudes;
Would-have-been studs structure the grid.
Everything opens to light and old winds:
Flushing and Bloodsuckers, Flensings and
    stragglers.

These will retire in tropical homes.

Meek

Time will come when the tyrants wane,
When Cape Cod will be encased in ice
Frozen like the final fires of hell
Where the tears of the taker confine.
To these Bible Belt complacent we say WOE
—
To Lexington's healthy horse breeders,
To Houston's oil oligarchs and their wives,
To St. Louis's stealers of farms
(The corn mutants of Monsanto fiefs),
To Indy's hoarders of insulin patents,
And redlining real-estate
Brokers spread like a patina of SPAM —
We say woe to you wicked Christians.
You feel secure in the coastless heights.
For Saudi and Iraq, for the Soviets and China.
For Mexico City and Singapore.
For Japan and Uganda, for Polynesia and
Sweden.
Are they so much worse for wear to insult?
Are you so better off than these beautiful
places?
And there will be time for The End to an-
guish greed.

When your lapis lazuli La-Z-Boys®
Fold inward in a fractured heap,
When the mojitos you inhale dockside
Slip in your sweat and shatter on deck,
When your Golden Globes gilded in Peru
mines
Tarnish by your misinvoiced trade policies,
When your Powers That Be lose your power
in three
Carefully placed hurricanes,
When your poor will be seen, empowered and
whole.
Enjoy your tours of juniper spirits,
Foodie reviews and festivals of music.
Enjoy your Costco wine and calves.
Your people — your poor — lie in ruin.
And because of that: America ain't great.

"If the civility of a society's what you want to
size,
Take a deeper look at its prisons." —Dos-
toevsky

The meal will get stripped to the bonemeal.
The lounge will stiffen, so languishes the sex,
And the market crashes making you the poor
And not merely the poor in meek spirit.

When your pride is ended, you will ask this:
How did the meek inherit the earth?

Dear Tolkien Society

It would take talent for Tolkien's dirge
Of Arthur and all the older knights
Of Camelot to receive the called-for response
Its original pages have rightly deserved —
The ending of ages, the altar of meter
Receiving a sacred sacrifice of devotion
Like Old English, alliterate and paced.

It would take the team of the Tolkien estate
Agreeing together that greater things
Could arise rightly from a ready pupil,
A published poet and pawn of the realm
Of the great and varied graves of scholastics
Who studied the song, who savored Gondor,
Who shun Shelob and shake with anger
At the mighty men molten Balrogs
Laid asunder in the lofty heights
Of the lowest dungeons and the lakes of ice.

It would take the tomes of Tolkien's notes

And a steady hand, studying longer,
And ready to write a rendered ending
Deserved by the start, daring to finish
What many have missed, what most wanted,
Yet still has never starred on the stud list
Of finished tales, of reforging swords,
That the master half-made before making
    a way
To the pearly gates and the price of life.

I would take the chance if you take me in.
I would write the end of the ruined saga.
I could give you the gold of the grave of the
    crown:
Pendragon's poem I dare to complete.

Storyweaving

I didn't know the nether spiders
Had woven these window panes with webs
New every night until the dawn
Sun had finished its ascent of the mount.

He flashed high beams in a flare at the pillar
And rocking chair and rich curtains
To limn the poem with gold light,
Slow pulsing like a pupal breath.

There in the panes is thankless weaving:
Strands of rhodium, strands of palladium,
Silvered rainbows thin as secrets,
Warping the windows into bright weft.

When I write again of storyweavers
You will know in part I yearn

For the myths that call the making angels
Who order the earths "eager spiders."

Healthy Shame

The greying mountains blushed again
As the bright birds bring songs
Of territory and tamer loves.
What a thing to think it song
When all they see is where
Another bird's boundary lies.
The mountain blushes with the merry water-
line of good Lake George.
For as it recedes in the early dawn
The spring mount — sprouting green
To accompany the conifers —
Wonders if it crossed a line at the wake.

Some things shout, "Don't steal my nest!"

Some things are so themselves
They blush at the slightest tidal splash.

Lines on Light

Some paint the light on the sheet,
Some paint by the side of the light,
But Dawn is uncaptured, dawn is loose.
Every other image and craft
Spellbinds your eyes and steals your light.
You look at a painting longing for prose,
You peer in a picture or part of a film,
You see a sculpture. But these aren't shining
For Dawn blinds the boys who rise
To greet her graces. She graves my mind,
My eyes, they're eager to avert off
To the side and write. Great streaks of
Blindness breaking those born clouds
And riddled ridges. If you see it rightly,
It is hard to stare at hardly at all.
She has wandered through the dark wood
Of the worlds and blackness to breach the
    Piedmont
And shine her torch sure in my retina,
Burning out a brazen, "There
You are my love! We have been looking
For you all night." She's yearning unseen,
How she fills the lines and figments with
    head-

Turning fusion of motes. How could you fake
As if this were ever thinkable in paint?

The Sun isn't something one can see.

But by her I see this happy verse,
Lines of light on lines of light or
Lines of light on lines of light.

The City is Recruited from the Country

Downstairs, my neighbor was stabbed today.
The cherry-bright Pepto Bismul
Glugged out of the mere gallon and a half
His forty-sixth year's frame
Had held within to be eaten by the snowbank
Or pool in the pavement of the Synagogue's
path.

There is no news outside needful:
Three assailants; searching for two;
Slashed on the hands; slit his face.
But was it a hate crime?
Or was it a lone wolf slasher?
Is there a difference these days?

I will not write this woe elsewhere.
If I blog about it, my buddies and mothers
Will write concerned. I'll have to unseal
Old demographic studies to prove to the dolts
That this kind of thing happens quite

Often — tenfold as often or more —
As it happens in my hood. But they don't
hear.

Perhaps it's because I merely have to call
Out "YO!" from where I'm looking, leaning
out my tower,
While they are shielded from local stabbings
By fences, walls, front yards,
And football games. I guarantee you:
It is not the city that is depraved anymore.

It wasn't for the early church, even,
But the country, the desert, the dark clouds
Rolling over the forbidden forest's ring
Of eldritch trees demanding a tryst
With sanguine knife sacrifice.
Neo-Pagan nihilism
Infects my city now, it seems,

But only cause of our murderous country.

Flying in Concrete

Imagine flying mid-concrete
C.D. Wright hath said, more or less.
New Yorkers have known this daily.
We are a people whose pedals move
As Huorns root; as hard waters;
As tentacular tubes of motion
Upon the grey gravelstone paths
That have not the healing powers
Of Roman limestone — seawater lithe
Powder and lith that liquid sunshine
Will heal whole. We have its cracks
As places to posture our promised dream.
We squirm along, squeal alone,
Squiggle in the sea of iron stones
For a splash of watercolor. For the rose spray
On the capstone where the stark hue
Of a carved maw — simulacrum —
Suggests something unthought:
Gargoyles are still good
When tamed and turned into a talisman.
You are now free to frolic in puddles
And gargle the rain; grey runners.

About Lancelot

Lancelot Schaubert has sold work to markets as diverse as MacMillan (TOR.-com), The New Haven Review (Yale's Institute Library), Nonbinary Review, Abyss and Apex, The Anglican Theological Review, 1632, B Cubed, McSweeney's, Writer's Digest, The World Series Edition of Poker Pro, Standard Publishing, the Poet's Market, and many, many similar markets. Spark + Echo selected him as their 2019 artist in residence, commissioning him to craft more than a dozen short fiction pieces.

He has ghostwritten and edited for NYT Bestsellers, written copy for large international nonprofit orgs and companies, and has served as an editor for bestselling fantasy authors Juliet Marillier, Kaaron Warren, and Howard Andrew Jones (for *Of Gods and Globes*). He also worked as a senior editor / producer for The Joplin Toad and Showbear Family Circus — the circus in its heyday published works from over 400 academics, authors, and artists.

As a producer and director-writer, he started out at fifteen in high school as a radio DJ and a regional thespian and never quite slowed down: he reinvented the photonovel through Cold Brewed with Mark Neuenschwander. That work caught the attention of the Missouri Tourism Board (as well as the Chicago Museum of Photography), who commissioned them to create a second photonovel, The Joplin Undercurrent. He also worked on films with Flying Treasure, WRKR, etc.. He helped judge the Brooklyn Film Festival and NYC Film Festival. And he wrote and produced the albums All Who Wander and H.A.L.T.S., both of which he performed in NYC venues like Rockwood Music Hall.

This all culminated in the narration of his first self-published audiobook, which Publisher's Weekly called "a hoot." Can also send audio samples of that or the albums.

He's currently on assignment in Alaska for a documentary film, in Brooklyn for a documentary film on the arts, a third in Brooklyn for a potential criminal justice story, and many other projects.

He lives and serves to help others make what they feel called to make.

Also by Lancelot Schaubert

- Substack essays and short fiction
- Of Gods and Globes I
- Of Gods and Globes II
- Of Gods and Globes III
- Bell Hammers: The True Folk Tale of Little Egypt — *historical humor novel*
- Tap & Die — *a "Die Bard" fantasy novella*
- 15 Vale Short Stories — *short stories from the universe where all of his fiction and nonfiction and poetry and photonovels connect*
- The Greenwood Poet — *poetry written during the pandemic in Greenwood cemetery, 500 acres of the oldest rural cemetery in America*
- Inconveniences Rightly Considered — *poems from his twenties*
- Harry Rides the Danger — *children's picture book on courage*
- The Elevator Out — *children's picture book on wonder*
- *H.A.L.T.S. — 90's alt-rock folk album*
- *All Who Wander — indie folk, experimental album*
- *Open — short film written for WRKR productions*
- *Cold Brewed — photo novel (graphic novel with still photographs) in a world where the prohibition made third wave coffee illegal*

Over at http://lanceschaubert.org you can find the archive of 400 academics, artists, and authors published in The Showbear Family Circus, resources for your own creative work, as well as ongoing serialized work by Lancelot.

Thanks for buying, reading, and sharing the work of living authors.

www.ingramcontent.com/pod-product-compliance
Lightning Source LLC
Chambersburg PA
CBHW030910060726
47591CB00005B/1486